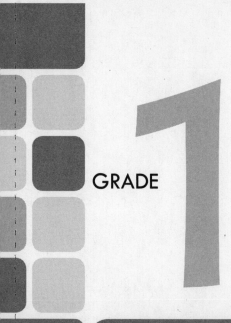

GRADE **1**

Foundational Skills
Workbook

PEARSON

Pearson Education, Inc., 330 Hudson Street, New York, NY 10013

Copyright © Pearson Education, Inc., or its affiliates. All Rights Reserved. Printed in the United States of America. This publication is protected by copyright, and permission should be obtained from the publisher prior to any prohibited reproduction, storage in a retrieval system, or transmission in any form or by any means, electronic, mechanical, photocopying, recording, or otherwise. The publisher hereby grants permission to reproduce pages, in part or in whole, for classroom use only, the number not to exceed the number of students in each class. Notice of copyright must appear on all copies. For information regarding permissions, request forms, and the appropriate contacts within the Pearson Education Global Rights & Permissions department, please visit www.pearsoned.com/permissions/.

PEARSON, ALWAYS LEARNING, and READYGEN are exclusive trademarks owned by Pearson Education, Inc. or its affiliates in the U.S. and/or other countries.

Unless otherwise indicated herein, any third-party trademarks that may appear in this work are the property of their respective owners and any references to third-party trademarks, logos, or other trade dress are for demonstrative or descriptive purposes only. Such references are not intended to imply any sponsorship, endorsement, authorization, or promotion of Pearson's products by the owners of such marks, or any relationship between the owner and Pearson Education, Inc. or its affiliates, authors, licensees, or distributors.

PEARSON

ISBN-13: 978-0-328-96298-3
ISBN-10:   0-328-96298-8

2   17

Phonics

© Pearson Education, Inc., 1

High-Frequency Words

Phonics Stories

© Pearson Education, Inc., 1

Name _____

Mm

Say the word for each picture.
Write m on the line if the word has the same first sound as .

1. _____

2. _____

3. _____

4. _____

5. _____

6. _____

7. _____

8. _____

© Pearson Education, Inc., 1

School + Home

Home Activity Your child has reviewed words that start with *m*. Help your child think of other words with /m/ as in *map*.

Ss

Say the word for each picture.
Write s on the line if the word has the same first sound as .

1. _____

2. _____

3. _____

4. _____

5. _____

6. _____

7. _____

8. _____

© Pearson Education, Inc., 1

School + Home

Home Activity Your child learned that some words begin with the letter *s*. Have your child find other words with /s/ as in *seal*.

© Pearson Education, Inc., 1

Name _____

Tt

Say the word for each picture.

Write t on the line if the word has the same first sound as a tiger.

1. _____

2. _____

3. _____

4. _____

5. _____

6. _____

7. _____

8. _____

School + Home **Home Activity** Your child learned that some words begin with the letter *t*. Have your child find other words with /t/ as in *tiger*.

3

Aa

Say the word for each picture.
Write a on the line if the word has the same first sound as

1.

2.

3.

4.

5.

6.

Say the word for each picture.
Write a on the line to complete the word.

© Pearson Education, Inc., 1

7.  **s** 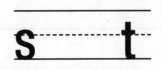 **t**   8. 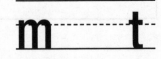 **m** ___ **t**

School + Home

Home Activity Your child learned about the short *a* vowel sound in words. Have your child find other words
with /a/ at the beginning or in the middle, such as *apple* and *pat*.

4

© Pearson Education, Inc., 1

Name _____

Cc

Say the word for each picture.
Write c on the line if the word has the same first sound as .

1.	2.
3.	4.
5.	6.
7.	8.

School + Home

Home Activity Your child learned that some words begin with the letter *c*. Have your child find other words with /k/ as in *cat*.

Pp

Say the word for each picture.
Write p on the line if the word has the same first sound as .

1. _____
2. _____
3. _____
4. _____

Say the word for each picture.
Write p on the line if the word has the same ending sound as .

5. ma _____
6. Sa _____
7. ca _____
8. sa _____

School + Home

Home Activity Your child learned that some words begin and end with the letter *p*. Have your child find other words that begin and end with /p/.

© Pearson Education, Inc., 1

Name _____

Nn

Say the word for each picture.

Write **n** on the line if the word has the same first sound as .

1.	2.
3.	4.

Say the word for each picture.

Write **n** on the line if the word has the same ending sound as .

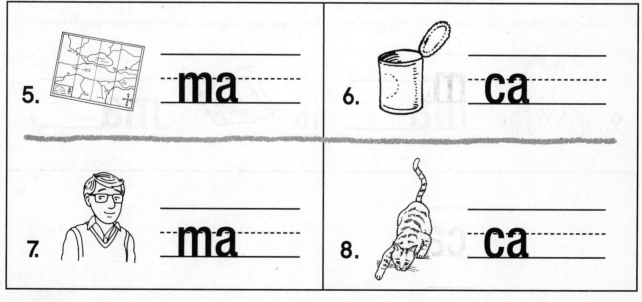

5. ma   6. ca

7. ma   8. ca

© Pearson Education, Inc., 1

Home Activity Your child learned that some words begin and end with the letter *n*. Have your child find other words that begin and end with /n/.

Name _____

Say the word for each picture.
Write the letter on the line that begins the word.

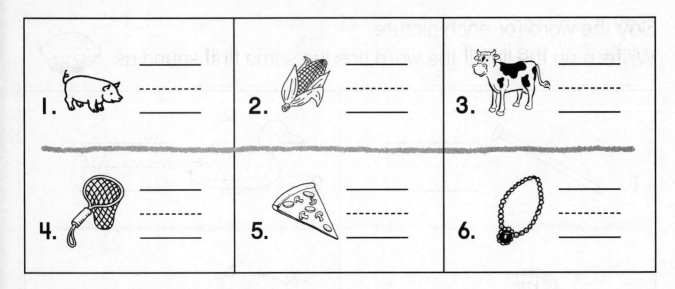

1. _____ _____
2. _____ _____
3. _____ _____
4. _____ _____
5. _____ _____
6. _____ _____

Write p or **n** on the line to complete the word.

7. ca _____
8. pa _____
9. ma _____
10. ma _____

© Pearson Education, Inc., 1

School + Home

Home Activity Your child reviewed words that begin with *c, n,* and *p* and reviewed words that end with *n* and *p*. Have your child find other words with /c/ as in *cat,* /p/ as in *pig,* and /n/ as in *nut.*

Name _____

Ff

Say the word for each picture.
Write **f** on the line if the word has the same first sound as .

1. _____	2. _____
3. _____	4. _____
5. _____	6. _____
7. _____	8. _____

© Pearson Education, Inc., 1

School + Home

Home Activity Your child learned that some words begin with the letter *f*. Have your child find other words with /f/ as in *fish*.

Bb

Say the word for each picture.
Write b on the line if the word has the same first sound as .

1. _____

2. _____

3. _____

4. _____

5. _____

6. _____

Write two words that rhyme with **nab**.

7. t _____

8. c _____

© Pearson Education, Inc., 1

School + Home

Home Activity Your child learned that some words begin and end with the letter *b*. Have your child find other words with /b/ as in *balloon*.

Name _____

Gg

Say the word for each picture.
Write **g** on the line if the word has the same first sound as .

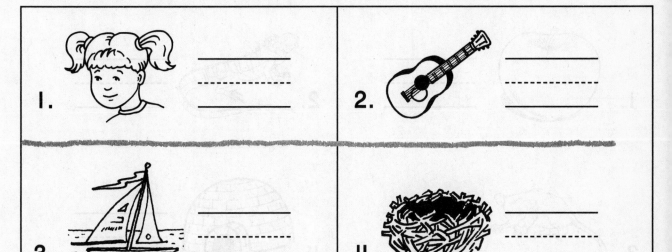

1.

2.

3.

4.

Write four words that rhyme with **gag**.

5. **s**

6. **n**

7. **t**

8. **b**

© Pearson Education, Inc., 1

Home Activity Your child has learned that some words begin and end with the letter *g*. Have your child find other words with /g/ as in *goat*. Work with your child to make words that rhyme with *gag*.

Ii

Say the word for each picture.
Write i on the line if the word has the same first sound as .

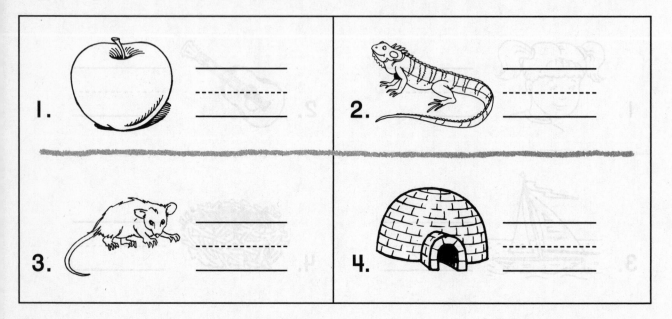

1. ___ ___
2. ___ ___
3. ___ ___
4. ___ ___

Say the word for each picture.
Write i on the line if the word has the same middle sound as .

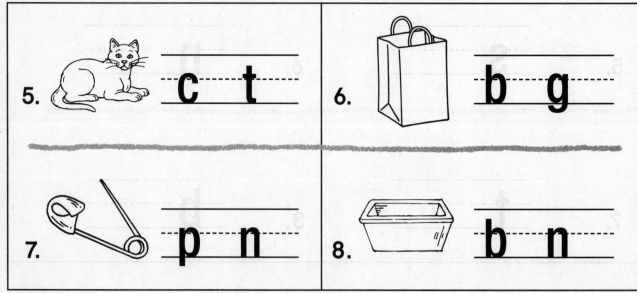

5. c ___ t
6. b ___ g
7. p ___ n
8. b ___ n

© Pearson Education, Inc., 1

School + Home

Home Activity Your child learned that some words have the short *i* sound. Have your child find other words with /i/ at the beginning or in the middle, such as *ink* and *sit*.

Dd

Say the word for each picture.

Write d on the line if the word has the same first sound as .

1.	2.
3.	4.

Say the word for each picture.

Write d on the line if the word has the same ending sound as .

5.	6.
7.	8.

© Pearson Education, Inc., 1

School + Home

Home Activity Your child learned that some words begin and end with the letter *d*. Have your child find other words that begin and end with /d/.

Name _____

L l

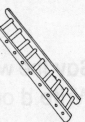

Say the word for each picture.
Write l on the line if the word has the same first sound as [ ].

1.  _____

2.  _____

3. _____

4.  _____

5.  _____

6.  _____

Write two words that rhyme with **pill**.

7. _____

8. _____

© Pearson Education, Inc., 1

School + Home

Home Activity Your child learned that some words begin with the letter *l*. Have your child find other words with /l/ as in *ladder*.

Name _____

Hh

Say the word for each picture.
Write **h** on the line if the word has the same first sound as .

1.	_ _ _ _ _	2.	_ _ _ _ _
3.	_ _ _ _ _	4.	_ _ _ _ _
5.	_ _ _ _ _	6.	_ _ _ _ _
7.	_ _ _ _ _	8.	_ _ _ _ _

© Pearson Education, Inc., 1

School + Home

Home Activity Your child learned that some words begin with the letter *h*. Have your child find other words with /h/ as in *helicopter*.

Name _____

Oo

Say the word for each picture.
Write o on the line if the word has the same first sound as .

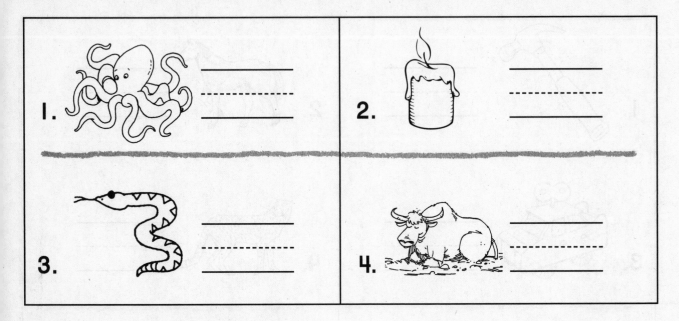

1. _____ / - - - - - -

2. _____ / - - - - - -

3. _____ / - - - - - -

4. _____ / - - - - - -

Say the word for each picture.
Write o on the line if the word has the same middle sound as ●.

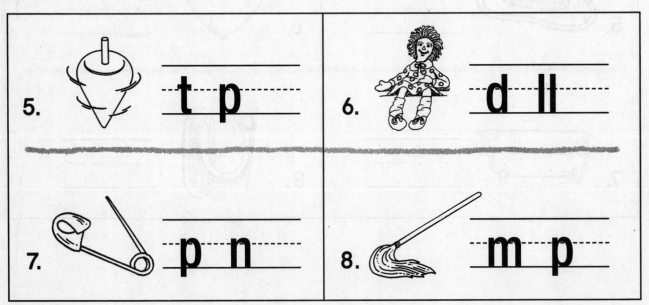

5. t ___ p

6. d ___ ll

7. p ___ n

8. m ___ p

© Pearson Education, Inc., 1

School + Home

Home Activity Your child learned about the short *o* vowel sound in words. Have your child find other words with /o/ at the beginning or in the middle, such as *octopus* and *box*.

Name _____

Rr

Say the word for each picture.
Write **r** on the line if the word has the same first sound as .

1. _____

2. _____

3. _____

4. _____

5. _____

6. _____

7. _____

8. _____

© Pearson Education, Inc., 1

School + Home

Home Activity Your child learned that some words begin with the letter *r*. Have your child find other words that begin with /r/ as in *rocket*.

Jj   Ww

Say the word for each picture.
Write j on the line if the word has the same first sound as .
Write w on the line if the word has the same first sound as .

1. _____

2. _____

3. _____

4. _____

5. _____

6. _____

7. _____

8. _____

© Pearson Education, Inc., 1

School + Home

Home Activity Your child learned that some words begin with the letter *w* and some words begin with the letter *j*. Have your child find other words that begin with /w/ as in *waterfall* and /j/ as in *jet*.

Name _____

Kk

Say the word for each picture.
Write **k** on the line if the word has the same first sound as .

1. _____ _____

2. _____ _____

3. _____ _____

4. _____ _____

5. _____ _____

6. _____ _____

Pick a word to finish each sentence.
Write the word on the line.

> Kim   kiss   kit

7. Sam will _____ Mom.

8. _____ will hit the rim with the .

© Pearson Education, Inc., 1

 School + Home

Home Activity Your child learned that some words begin with the letter *k*. Have your child find other words that begin with /k/ as in *kitten*.

Name _____

Ee

Say the word for each picture.
Write e on the line if the word has the same first sound as .

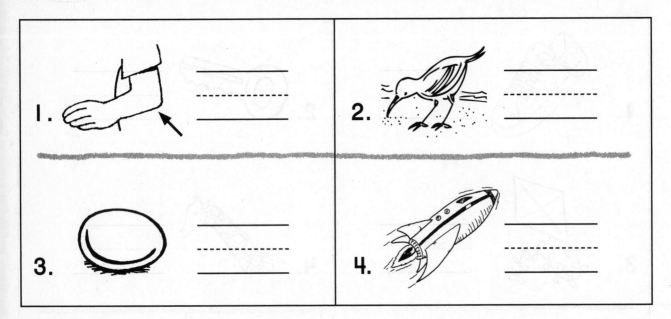

1.

2.

3.

4.

Say the word for each picture.
Write e on the line if the word has the same middle sound as .

5.

6.

7.

8.

© Pearson Education, Inc., 1

Home Activity Your child learned that some words have the short *e* sound. Have your child find other words with /e/ at the beginning or in the middle, such as *elephant* and *bell*.

Name _____

Vv

Say the word for each picture.
Write v on the line if the word has the same first sound as .

1.	_____ ------- _____	2.	_____ ------- _____
3.	_____ ------- _____	4.	_____ ------- _____
5.	_____ ------- _____	6.	_____ ------- _____

Write V or v to make a word.

7. ___**at**___

8. ___**ic**___

9. ___**al**___

10. ___**an**___

© Pearson Education, Inc., 1

Home Activity Your child learned that some words begin with the letter *v*. Have your child find other words with /v/ as in *volcano*.

Name _____

Yy   Zz

Say the word for each picture.
Write **y** on the line if the word has the same first sound as .
Write **z** on the line if the word has the same first sound as 🦓 .

1. ⭕ _____	2. 🐻 _____
3. 🔩 _____	4. 🏠 _____
5. ⛺ _____	6. 🐂 _____
7. 🎁 _____	8. 🧶 _____

© Pearson Education, Inc., 1

School + Home

Home Activity Your child learned that some words begin with *y* and some words begin with *z*. Have your child find other words that begin with /y/ as in *yo-yo* and /z/ as in *zebra*.

Name _____

Uu

Say the name of the picture.
Write **u** on the line if the word has the same first sound as

1. _____ - - - - - - -	2. _____ - - - - - - -
3. _____ - - - - - - -	4. _____ - - - - - - -

Say the name of the picture.
Write **u** on the line if the word has the same middle sound as

.

5. s n	6. t b
7. b g	8. p n

© Pearson Education, Inc., 1

Home Activity Your child learned about the short *u* vowel sound in words. Have your child find other words that have the same sound as /u/ at the beginning or in the middle, such as *umbrella* and *rug*.

Name _____

Qq

Say the word for each picture.
Write **q** on the line if the word has the same first sound as .

1.  _ _ _ _ _ _	2.  _ _ _ _ _ _
3.  _ _ _ _ _ _	4. _ _ _ _ _ _
5.  _ _ _ _ _ _	6.  _ _ _ _ _ _

Write **qu** to make a word.

7. _ _ _ _ _ **ilt**

8. _ _ _ _ _ **it**

9. _ _ _ _ _ **iz**

10. _ _ _ _ _ **ick**

© Pearson Education, Inc., 1

Home Activity Your child learned that some words begin with the letter *q*. Have your child find other words that begin with /kw/ as in *quilt*.

24

Name _____

Say the word for each picture.
Write a on the line if you hear the **short a** sound.

c<u>a</u>t

1.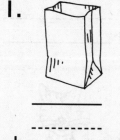
b _____ g

2.
f _____ n

3.
m _____ p

4.
m _____ p

5.
c _____ n

6.
m _____ n

7.
p _____ g

8.
v _____ n

Write a word for each picture.

9.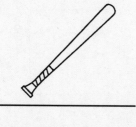
_____

10.
_____

© Pearson Education, Inc., 1

School + Home

Home Activity Your child has reviewed words with the short *a* sound heard in *cat*. Work with your child to make words that rhyme with *cat* and *man*.

25

Name _____

Say the word for each picture.
Write ck on the line if the word has the same ending sound as .

1.	2. 	3.	4. 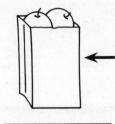
ta _____	ba _____	fa _____	sa _____

5. 	6. 	7. 	8. 
ha _____	ja _____	pa _____	ca _____

Write two words that have the same ending sound as .

_____   _____

- - - - - - - - - - - - - - - -

_____   _____

© Pearson Education, Inc., 1

School + Home

Home Activity Your child practiced reading and creating words that end in *ck*. Help your child write words that rhyme with *sack*.

26

Name _____

Say the word for each picture.
Write i on the line if you hear the **short i** sound.

p<u>i</u>g

---

1. _____

k _____ ck

2. _____

h _____ ll

3. _____

t _____ ck

4. _____

f _____ n

---

5. _____

p _____ n

6. _____

d _____ g

7. _____

w _____ g

8. _____

z _____ p

Circle the word to finish each sentence. **Write** it on the line.

9. _____

I _____ go.

will   wall

10. _____

Sam _____ the mat.

hip   hid

© Pearson Education, Inc., 1

School + Home

Home Activity Your child practiced creating words with the short *i* sound heard in *pig*. Help your child make up fun rhymes using short *i* words, such as *The big pig in the wig can dig and do a jig.*

27

Name _____

Say the word for each picture.
Write x on the line if the word has the same
ending sound as **ax**.

a<u>x</u>

---

1. 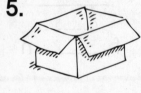	2. 	3. 	4.
si _____	wa _____	li _____	ki _____

5.	6. 	7.	8. 
bo _____	mi _____	si _____	fi _____

Write two words that have the same ending sound as **6**.

_____   _____

- - - - - - - - - - - - - - - - - - -   - - - - - - - - - - - - - - - - - - -

Read the sentence below. **Underline** the words that have the
same ending sound as **ax**.

He saw six wax cats.

© Pearson Education, Inc., 1

School + Home **Home Activity** Your child practiced creating words that end with *x*. Write *six*, *mix*, and *fix* on cards. Have your child choose a card, read the word, and use it in a sentence.

Name _____

Say the word for each picture.
Circle the picture if the word has
the short o sound you hear in top.

t<u>o</u>p

1.

2.

3.

4.

5.

6.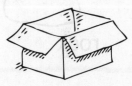

7.

8.

9.

10.

11.

12.

13.

14.

15.

© Pearson Education, Inc., 1

School + Home

Home Activity Your child practiced creating words with the short o sound heard in *top*. Encourage your child to use the short o words pictured above in sentences.

29

Name _____

Circle a word to match each picture.

pan**s**

1.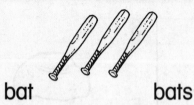

bat   bats

2.

mop   mops

3.

rock   rocks

4.

pig   pigs

5.

top   tops

6.

cap   caps

7.

kit   kits

8.

sack   sacks

Write a sentence for each word.

9. cats _____

10. wigs _____

© Pearson Education, Inc., 1

School + Home

Home Activity Your child identified singular and plural nouns. Have your child name items around the house. Point out the use of *-s* at the end of many plural words, such as *books, apples,* and *bowls.*

Name _____

Add -s to each word.
Write the new word on the line.

1. hop _____

2. sit _____

3. see _____

4. pat _____

5. help _____

Use the words you wrote to finish the sentences.
Write the words on the lines.

6. Jack _____ a big dog.

7. Jack _____ the dog.

8. Jack _____ on a rock.

9. The dog _____ Jack.

10. The dog _____ on Jack.

Home Activity Your child added -s to verbs. Have your child write the verbs *see, fan, nap, dig, sit, hop, jog,* and *mop,* and add an -s to each verb. Have your child pick a verb and use it in a sentence about you, such as *Mommy hops.* Then act out the sentence.

© Pearson Education, Inc., 1

31

Name _____

Add -ing to each word.
Write the new word on the line.

_____

1. help _____

_____

2. look _____

_____

3. fix _____

_____

4. lick _____

_____

5. play _____

Use the words you wrote to finish the sentences.
Write the words on the lines.

_____

6. Jan is _____ at the cats.

_____

7. Jan is _____ the cats.

_____

8. The cats are _____ with the can.

_____

9. The big cat is _____ the little cat.

_____

10. Jan is _____ the lock.

Home Activity Your child added -ing to verbs. Have your child write the verbs *lick, rock, kick, eat,* and *mix* on slips of paper. Then have your child add -ing to each verb. Have your child pick a slip of paper and act out the word for you to guess.

© Pearson Education, Inc., 1

Name _____

Circle the word for each picture.

w<u>e</u>b

1.

mitt   men   man

2.

bed   bid   bad

3.

pen   pan   pin

4. **10**

tin   tan   ten

5.

jam   jet   jog

6.

net   not   nip

Circle the word the completes each sentence.

7. The fat _____ sits on my lap.

hen   hat

8. I like my short _____ hat.

rid   red

© Pearson Education, Inc., 1

School + Home

Home Activity Your child practiced reading words with the short *e* sound heard in *web*. Work with your child to make words that rhyme with *pet* or *bell*.

Name _____

Pick letters from the box to finish each word.
Write the letters on the line.

 **sw**im

| bl | cl | cr | dr | fl | fr | gr | sl | sm | st |

1. _____ag

2. _____ock

3. _____ap

4. _____ess

5. _____ab

6. _____og

7. _____ell

8. _____ed

9. _____ep

10. _____in

© Pearson Education, Inc., 1

School + Home

Home Activity Your child practiced creating words with initial blends (*flag, dress, sled*). Help your child make up silly sentences that each contain words beginning with just one blend, such as *Freddy frog likes French fries*.

Name _____

Say the word for each picture.
Write u on the line if you hear the **short u** sound.

p<u>u</u>p

1.

b _____ g

2.

d _____ ck

3.

b _____ s

4.

h _____ g

5.

b _____ x

6.

dr _____ m

7.

s _____ n

8.

sl _____ d

Write a sentence for each word.

_____

9. mud _____

_____

10. plum _____

© Pearson Education, Inc., 1

Home Activity Your child identified and created words with the short *u* sound heard in *pup*. Work with your child to write words that rhyme with *rug*.

35

Name _____

Say the word for each picture.
Circle the letters that finish each word.
Write the letters on the line.

ne**st**

---

nd   nt

1. po _____

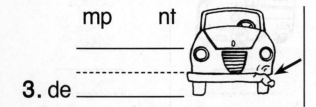

nt   mp

2. ju _____

---

mp   nt

3. de _____

st   nt

4. ca _____

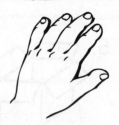

---

st   mp

5. la _____

nt   nd

6. ha _____

---

st   nt

7. ve _____

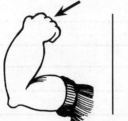

nt   mp

8. te _____

---

nt   st

9. fi _____

mp   st

10. sta _____

© Pearson Education, Inc., 1

School + Home

Home Activity Your child created words using final consonant blends such as *mp, nd, nt,* and *st*. Have your child make up sentences using words from this page.

Name _____

Say the word for each picture.
Write sh or **th** to finish each word.

di**sh**   **th**ink

---

1. _____
   _____ op

2. _____
   fi _____

---

3. _____
   _____ in

4. _____
   _____ ell

---

5. _____
   ba _____

6. _____
   bru _____

Circle a word to finish each sentence. **Write** the word.

path   math

_____
_____

7. She walked on the bike _____ .

---

drip   ship

_____
_____

8. I saw the _____ from the beach.

© Pearson Education, Inc., 1

School + Home

Home Activity Your child added the digraphs *sh* and *th* (two letters that together stand for one sound) to complete words. Have your child copy the words that contain *sh* from this page and use as many of those words as possible in one sentence. Repeat using the *th* words.

Name _____

Circle a word to finish each sentence.
Write it on the line.

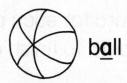 b**a**ll

---

mall   mill

_____

- - - - - - - - - - - - - - - -

1. We met Dad at the _____.

---

well   walk

_____

- - - - - - - - - - - - - - - -

2. We take a _____ and talk.

---

tell   tall

_____

- - - - - - - - - - - - - - - -

3. Dad got a _____ bag.

---

all   ill

_____

- - - - - - - - - - - - - - - -

4. We _____ go in.

---

smell   small

_____

- - - - - - - - - - - - - - - -

5. I am too _____ to see!

© Pearson Education, Inc., 1

School + Home

Home Activity Your child practiced reading words with the vowel sound heard in *ball* and *walk*. Work with your child to write a list of words that rhyme with *ball*.

38

Name _____

Circle the word for each picture.

 c<u>a</u>ke

---

1.

rake   rack

2.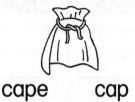

snack   snake

3.

frog   frame

4.

can   cane

5.

cape   cap

6.

plane   plan

Choose a word to finish each sentence. **Write** the word on the line.

lake   lock

7. I like to swim in the _____.

plant   plate

8. Please put the food on the _____.

gum   game

9. Will you play this _____ with me?

gate   skate

10. I can _____ fast.

© Pearson Education, Inc., 1

 School + Home

Home Activity Your child practiced reading words with the long *a* sound spelled *a _ e,* such as *cake.* Work with your child to write a list of words that rhyme with *cake.* Repeat with *cave.*

Name _____

Circle the word for each picture.
Write it on the line.

 lac**e**

 a**g**e

---

1.

face   fake

_____

- - - - - - - - - - - -

2.

rake   race

_____

- - - - - - - - - - - -

3.

cave   cage

_____

- - - - - - - - - - - -

4.

wag   wage

_____

- - - - - - - - - - - -

5.

speck   space

_____

- - - - - - - - - - - -

6.

stage   stake

_____

- - - - - - - - - - - -

7.

track   trace

_____

- - - - - - - - - - - -

8.

pace   page

_____

- - - - - - - - - - - -

Circle the word to finish each sentence. **Write** the word.

lace   brake

_____

- - - - - - - - - - - - - - - -

9. I tripped on my _____ .

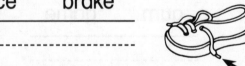

page   cage

_____

- - - - - - - - - - - - - - - -

10. My pet bird lives in a _____ .

Home Activity Your child practiced reading and writing words that have the sound that *c* stands for in *lace* and the sound that *g* stands for in *age*. Ask your child to write a list of words that rhyme with *lace* and a list of words that rhyme with *age*.

© Pearson Education, Inc., 1

Name _____

Circle the word for each picture.

1. 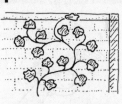	2. 	3. 	4. 
vine　vane	mane　mice	wig　wipe	bike　bill

Say the name of each picture.
Write the letters to finish each word.

5. 	6. 	7. 	8. 
_ _ _ _ _ _	_ _ _ _ _ _	_ _ _ _ _ _	_ _ _ _ _ _

Pick a word to finish each sentence. **Write** the word on the line.

slice　　price

_____

9. I bought a _____ of pizza.

bite　　rice

_____

10. "Would you like a _____?" I asked.

© Pearson Education, Inc., 1

School + Home **Home Activity** Your child practiced reading words with the long *i* sound spelled *i _ e*, such as *nine*. Work with your child to write a list of words that rhyme with *nine*. Repeat with *hide*.

Name _____

Circle the word for each picture.

 <u>wh</u>isk   **ch**ick    <u>itch</u>

| 1.  wall   whale | 2.  shin   chin | 3.  catch   cats | 4.  wash   watch |

| 5.  ship   whip | 6.  chick   check | 7.  patch   pass | 8. limp   chimp |

Pick a word to finish each sentence. **Write** the word on the line.

graph   grass

_____

- - - - - - - - - - - - - - - - - -

9. Henry made a mistake on his _____ .

what   want

_____

- - - - - - - - - - - - - - - - - -

10. He did not know _____ to do.

© Pearson Education, Inc., 1

Home Activity Your child practiced reading words with digraphs *wh, ch,* and *tch* (letters that together stand for one sound). Have your child use each word above in a sentence.

School + Home

Name _____

Write the letters to make a word in each sentence.
Then read the story.

 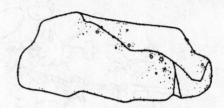 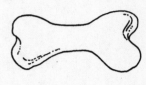

R __ __ s __ __ wanted to make soup. She didn't have a

b __ __ n __ __ . So she put a big **st** __ __ n __ __ in the pot. She

didn't have a **st** __ __ v __ __ . She made a fire outside her

h __ __ m __ __ . She hung the pot on a **p** __ __ l __ __ .

"I **h** __ __ **p** __ __ this will be good," Rose said.

Circle the words that have the same long o sound as .

clove   bond   not   poke   stop   spoke

drop   lost   vote   son   color   told

© Pearson Education, Inc., 1

School + Home
Home Activity Your child practiced reading words with the long o sound spelled o – e, such as rope. Work with your child to write a list of words that rhyme with bone. Repeat with joke.

Name _____

Read each sentence.
Write the contraction for the underlined words.

I <u>**do not**</u> think I can do this.   I <u>**don't**</u> think I can do this.

_____

1. "I <u>**can not**</u> make a nest," said the little bird.   _____

2. "I <u>will</u> need help with the sticks," said
   the little bird.   _____

3. "I <u>do not</u> think I can help," said the frog.   _____

4. "<u>You will</u> need a big bird to help you,"
   said the frog.   _____

5. "<u>I am</u> a big bird! I can help," said
   the big bird.   _____

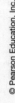

© Pearson Education, Inc., 1

School + Home

Home Activity Your child combined words to form contractions ending with *n't, 'm,* and *'ll*. Say a contraction aloud. Have your child tell you the two words that were combined to make the contraction. Repeat with the other contractions.

Name _____

Circle the word for each picture.

 c<u>u</u>be

1.

mule   mile

2.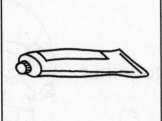

tub   tube

3.

cub   cube

4.

Pete   pet

5.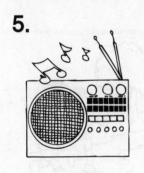

tug   tune

6.

flat   flute

7.

tub   tube

8.

hug   huge

Find the word that has the same **long u** sound as  .
Mark the ⬭ to show your answer.

9. ⬭ rut
   ⬭ rid
   ⬭ rule

10. ⬭ cut
    ⬭ cute
    ⬭ cup

© Pearson Education, Inc., 1

 School + Home

Home Activity Your child practiced reading words with the long *u* sound spelled *u – e*, such as *cube*. Write words from this page in a list. Say each word. Have your child point to the word and read it.

Name _____

Pick a word from the box to finish each sentence.
Add -ed to each word. **Write** it on the line.

| call   walk   sniff   jump   rest |

_____
- - - - - - - - - - - - - - - - - -
1. They _____ rope together.

_____
- - - - - - - - - - - - - - - - - -
2. Pam _____ June.

_____
- - - - - - - - - - - - - - - - - -
3. They _____ to the park.

_____
- - - - - - - - - - - - - - - - - -
4. They _____ in the shade.

_____
- - - - - - - - - - - - - - - - - -
5. They _____ the flowers.

Home Activity Your child practiced writing words ending in -ed, such as patched. Ask your child to read each word and use it in a sentence.

46

© Pearson Education, Inc., 1

Name _____

Help the bee get home.
Read each word.
Draw a line that goes past only the **long e** words.
Write the **long e** words on the lines.

b<u>ee</u>

feet

bed

beet

wet

sheet

we

net

peel

jeep

he

jet   me

Home

1. _____

2. _____

3. _____

4. _____

5. _____

6. _____

7. _____

8. _____

© Pearson Education, Inc., 1

School + Home

Home Activity Your child practiced reading and writing words with the long *e* sound spelled *e* and *ee*, as in *he* and *jeep*. Have your child make a list of words that rhyme with *seed*. Repeat with *jeep*.

47

Name _____

Circle the word for each picture.

 <u>kitt</u>en

---

1.

ramp   rabbit

2.

button   brake

3.

dinner   dent

4.

base   basket

5.

helmet   hello

6.

napkin   name

7.

mask   muffin

8.

wall   walnut

Draw a picture for each word.

9. mitten

10. picnic

© Pearson Education, Inc., 1

School + Home

Home Activity Your child read words with two syllables that have two consonants in the middle, as in *kitten*. Have your child choose five words from the page and use each word in a sentence.

48

Name _____

   fry

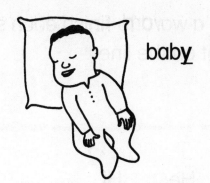   baby

Circle the word for each picture.

1.	2.	3.	4.
puppy put	flop fly	muddy meet	bunny ball

5.	6.	7.	8.
crib cry	sit city	sky skate	had happy

Circle the word to finish each sentence. **Write** it on the line.

_____

9. I didn't eat breakfast and I was very _____.
   hungry money

_____

10. After a day at the beach, my bathing suit was not _____.
    dry my

© Pearson Education, Inc., 1

School + Home **Home Activity** Your child practiced reading words with the vowel sounds of *y* heard in *fry* or *baby*. Work with your child to put the above answers into two word lists—one of words in which *y* represents the long *e* sound (*baby*) and one in which it represents the long *i* sound (*fry*).

Name _____

Circle a word to finish each sentence.
Write it on the line.

 n<u>o</u>

He   Hi

_____

- - - - - - - - - - - - - - - - - - -

1. "_____," Luke said.

Hi   He

_____

- - - - - - - - - - - - - - - - - - -

2. _____ is little.

No   Nod

_____

- - - - - - - - - - - - - - - - - - -

3. _____ one can see him.

---

so   see

_____

- - - - - - - - - - - - - - - - - - -

4. She is _____ big.

---

bed   be

_____

- - - - - - - - - - - - - - - - - - -

5. He will grow to _____ big too.

© Pearson Education, Inc., 1

 School + Home

Home Activity Your child practiced reading words with the long vowel pattern heard in *me, hi,* and *go.* Work with your child to make a list of words with the long *e* sound spelled *e* and the long *o* sound spelled *o.*

Name _____

 r**ing**
 ba**nk**

Circle the word for each picture.

1. sink   sing

2. skunk   skate

3. sink   side

4. kink   king

5. wink   wing

6. trunk   truck

7. hand   hang

8. swim   swing

Write the letters **ng** or **nk** to finish the words for each sentence.

9. Please b r i ___ ___ me a d r i ___ ___.

10. T h a ___ ___ you for the pretty r i ___ ___.

11. I heard the horn h o ___ ___.

© Pearson Education, Inc., 1

 School + Home   **Home Activity** Your child read words that end with *ng* and *nk*. Say one of the words with *ng* or *nk* on this page and ask your child to say a word that rhymes with it. Then have your child say a word for you to rhyme.

Name _____

Pick a word from the box to finish each compound word.
Write it on the line.
Draw a line to the picture it matches.

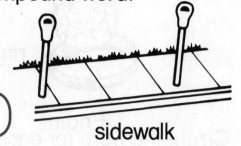

ball   cakes   pole   set

sidewalk

1. pan _____

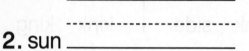

2. sun _____

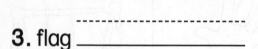

3. flag _____

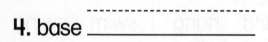

4. base _____

Find the compound word.
Mark the ⬭ to show your answer.

5. ⬭ sandy   6. ⬭ napkin
   ⬭ sandman   ⬭ happen
   ⬭ sanding   ⬭ dishpan

© Pearson Education, Inc., 1

Home Activity Your child read compound words—words formed by joining two or more other words. Walk around your house with your child and find things you see that are compound words *(toothbrush, hairbrush, bathtub)*. Say each word and have your child identify the two words used to make the compound word.

Name _____

Greg fix<u>es</u> the bench<u>es</u>.

Add the ending.
Write the new word on the line.

Word	Ending	New Word
1. mix	+ -es	
2. brush	+ -es	
3. glass	+ -es	
4. catch	+ -es	
5. dress	+ -es	
6. bus	+ -es	
7. dish	+ -es	
8. fox	+ -es	
9. nut	+ -s	
10. patch	+ -es	

© Pearson Education, Inc., 1

School + Home

Home Activity Your child added -es to verbs and nouns. Have your child use each new word in a sentence.

Name _____

Circle the word for each picture.

 st**or**m

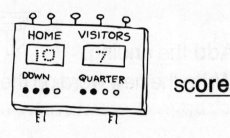 sc**ore**

1.

fork　flick

2.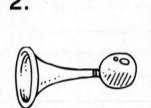

hen　horn

3.

core　conk

4.

store　stock

5.

con　corn

6.

shorts　shots

7.

port　pot

8.

thorn　tone

Find the word that has the same middle sound as   .
Mark the ⬭ to show your answer.

9. ⬭ porch
　⬭ poke
　⬭ pole

10. ⬭ such
　⬭ shut
　⬭ shore

© Pearson Education, Inc., 1

 Home Activity Your child read words with *or* as in *storm* and *ore* as in *score*. Help your child make up a story using words with this vowel sound, such as *snore, horn, popcorn,* and *short.* Then have your child illustrate his or her story.

Name _____

Dan is mop**ping** up the mess.
The mess is mop**ped** up.

Add -ed and **-ing** to each word.
Write the new words on the lines.

	Add -ed	**Add -ing**
1. nap		
2. pat		
3. nod		
4. jog		
5. wag		
6. stop		
7. pet		
8. drop		
9. clap		
10. plan		

© Pearson Education, Inc., 1

School + Home

Home Activity Your child practiced writing words that end in -ed and -ing. Together with your child make up a story using the words above.

Name _____

Circle the word for each picture.

 **farm**

1.	2.	3.	4.
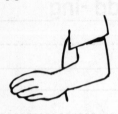			
arm am	band barn	core car	far jam

5.	6.	7.	8.

duck dark	party patty	cart cork	cord card

Find the word that rhymes with ☆.
Mark the ⬭ to show your answer.

9. ⬭ form
   ⬭ far
   ⬭ for

10. ⬭ tar
    ⬭ torn
    ⬭ trap

© Pearson Education, Inc., 1

 School + Home
Home Activity Your child read words with *ar* as in *farm*. Help your child make up a story about a car trip. Encourage your child to use words with *ar* that have the same vowel sound as *car*.

Name _____

h**er**   b**ir**d   s**ur**f

Circle the word for each picture.

1. 	2. 	3. 	4. 
short shirt	clerk click	curl chill	barn burn

5. 	6. 	7. 	8. 
fern fan	skirt skit	fist first	stir store

Find the word that has the same vowel sound as .
Mark the ⬭ to show your answer.

9. ⬭ hard
⬭ hut
⬭ hurt

10. ⬭ torn
⬭ turn
⬭ tune

© Pearson Education, Inc., 1

Home Activity Your child read words spelled with *er, ir,* and *ur* that have the same vowel sound as *bird*.
Help your child make up rhymes using words with this vowel sound spelled *er, ir, ur*. For example,
You can't wear that shirt. It is covered in dirt!

Name _____

Pick a word from the box that means the same as each pair of words. **Write** it on the line.

<u>She is</u> tall.
<u>She's</u> tall.

he's	it's	I've	that's	they're
they've	we're	we've	you're	you've

1. I + have

_____

__ __ __ __ __ __ __ __

_____

2. we + are

_____

__ __ __ __ __ __ __ __

_____

3. it + is

_____

__ __ __ __ __ __ __ __

_____

4. that + is

_____

__ __ __ __ __ __ __ __

_____

5. you + have

_____

__ __ __ __ __ __ __ __

_____

6. they + have

_____

__ __ __ __ __ __ __ __

_____

7. we + have

_____

__ __ __ __ __ __ __ __

_____

8. he + is

_____

__ __ __ __ __ __ __ __

_____

9. they + are

_____

__ __ __ __ __ __ __ __

_____

10. you + are

_____

__ __ __ __ __ __ __ __

_____

© Pearson Education, Inc., 1

School + Home

Home Activity Your child practiced making contractions with *'s, 've,* and *'re.* Read each contraction on this page aloud. Challenge your child to use each one in a sentence. Then work together to write each sentence.

58

Name _____

Circle the word for each picture.

small   small**er**   small**est**

1.

faster   fastest

2.

bigger   biggest

3.

taller   tallest

4.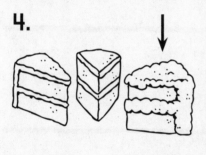

sweeter   sweetest

5.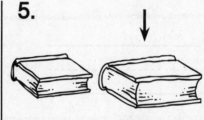

thicker   thickest

6.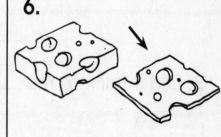

thinner   thinnest

Write -er or **-est** to finish the word in each sentence.

7. The little bird has the few _____ eggs.

8. The little bird has a long _____ tail than the big bird.

© Pearson Education, Inc., 1

 Home Activity Your child identified the comparative endings -er and -est as in *smaller* and *smallest*. Discuss the sizes, shapes, and colors of animals. Have your child compare the animals using -er when comparing two and -est when comparing more than two.

Name _____

Read each word in the box. **Pick** a word from the box to finish each sentence. **Write** it on the line. **Read** each completed sentence.

| fudge | hedge | judge | ledge | smudge |

ba**dge**

_____
1. Mom made _____ for us to eat.

_____
2. She set it on the _____ .

_____
3. Did it fall into the _____ ?

_____
4. Look, there's a _____ on Bear's face.

_____
5. The _____ thinks Bear ate it too.

© Pearson Education, Inc., 1

Home Activity Your child learned to read words that end with -dge that have the sound heard in *judge*. Have your child make a list of words that rhyme with *judge*.

Name  _____

t**ai**l →

pl**ay**

Circle the word for each picture.

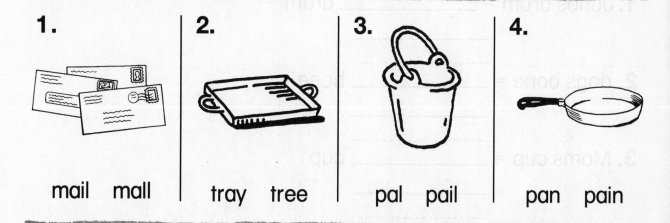

1.	2.	3.	4.
mail mall	tray tree	pal pail	pan pain

5.	6.	7.	8.
sell sail	he hay	train trap	page pay

Find the word that has the same **long a** sound as  .
Mark the ⬭ to show your answer.

9. ⬭ clip
⬭ clap
⬭ clay

10. ⬭ man
⬭ main
⬭ mine

© Pearson Education, Inc., 1

Home Activity Your child read words in which the long *a* sound is spelled *ai* and *ay*, as in *rain* and *hay*. Ask your child to name a rhyming word for each long *a* word on this page.

Name _____

Write each word correctly.
Use **'s** or **'** at the end of each word.

Meg**'s** hat

_____

1. Janes drum = _____ drum

_____

2. dogs bone = _____ bone

_____

3. Moms cup = _____ cup

_____

4. babys crib = _____ crib

_____

5. pets beds = _____ beds

Pick a word from the box to match each picture.
Write it on the line.

| girls'   Matt's |

_____

6. _____ lunch

_____

7. _____ games

© Pearson Education, Inc., 1

Home Activity Your child wrote words that show ownership. Point out objects in your home that are owned by one or more persons in the family. Ask your child to use a possessive to tell you who owns each object (*Mike's pen*).

Name _____

Circle the word for each picture.

1.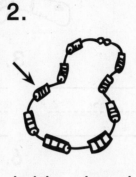

head   herd

2.

bride   bead

3.

sail   seal

4.

berry   bread

5.

leaf   loaf

6.

jeans   jars

7.

bake   beak

8.

clean   clang

Circle the words that finish each sentence.

9. **Please/Place** pass the **peas/bees**.

10. I **spread/spent** the jam on the cracker.

11. I **read /rang** my book at the **beach/birch** yesterday.

Home Activity Your child read words in which both short *e* and long *e* sounds are spelled *ea*. Ask your child to think of rhyming words for the words on this page. Write word and review the spelling together.

© Pearson Education, Inc., 1

63

Name _____

Add -ed to each word.
Write the new word on the line.

fr**ied**

1. dry

_____

- - - - - - - - - - - - - -

2. cry

_____

- - - - - - - - - - - - - -

3. spy

_____

- - - - - - - - - - - - - -

4. worry

_____

- - - - - - - - - - - - - -

5. try

_____

- - - - - - - - - - - - - -

6. copy

_____

- - - - - - - - - - - - - -

Add -er and **-est** to each word.
Write the new word on the lines.

	Add -er	**Add -est**
7. silly		
8. funny		
9. happy		
10. easy		

School + Home

Home Activity Your child practiced adding endings to words where the spelling changed from *y* to *i* before adding *-ed*, *-er*, or *-est*. Use the words above to make up a story with your child.

64

© Pearson Education, Inc., 1

Name _____

Circle the word for each picture.

t**oa**d   bl**ow**

1.	2.	3.	4.
snap snow	road rod	boat beat	sap soap

5.	6.	7.	8.
bee bow	coat cot	ray row	leaf loaf

Write the letters that finish the words in each sentence.

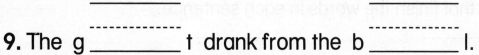

9. The g _____ t drank from the b _____ l.

10. They looked high and l _____ but they could not find the

r _____ d.

Home Activity Your child created and read words in which the long *o* sound is spelled *oa* and *ow*, as in *toad* and *blow*. Together, list as many words as possible with the long *o* sound in their names. Then ask your child to sort the words by their spellings.

© Pearson Education, Inc., 1

Name _____

Circle the word for each picture.

1.
stub
scrub

2.
splash
slash

3.
squeeze
sneeze

4.
sting
string

5.
lint
splint

6.
spring
sing

7. **3**
those
three

8.
stripe
ripe

Write the letters that finish the words in each sentence.

9. She _____ e w the ball _____ o u g h the

_____ e e n door.

10. I had a sore _____ o a t.

© Pearson Education, Inc., 1

School + Home
Home Activity Your child created and read words that begin with three-letter consonant blends. Have your child draw pictures of *screen, spray, squint,* and *street.* Have him or her label each picture with the word.

66

Phonics

Name _____

Circle the word for each picture.

1.	2.	3.	4.
night note	sit lie	tie tea	fit fight

5.	6.	7.	8.
pit pie	hay high	sit sight	tight toad

Read the sentences.
Circle the words that have the **long i** sound spelled **ie** and **igh**.
Underline the words that have the **long e** sound spelled **ie**.

9. I would like another piece of birthday cake.

10. He believes that he is right.

11. I am sorry that I lied to you.

Home Activity Your child practiced reading words in which the long *i* sound is spelled *igh* and *ie* as in *light* and *pie*, and words in which the long *e* sound is spelled *ie*. Encourage your child to create a poem, nonsense rhyme, or song using *igh* and *ie* words.

© Pearson Education, Inc., 1

Name _____

Circle the word for each picture.

knight   **wr**ench

1.

knife   night

2.

rest   wrist

3.

nine   knit

4.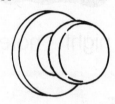

knob   not

5.

note   knot

6.

wreck   rack

7.

white   write

8.

ring   wrong

Find the word that has the same beginning sound as the picture.
Mark the ⬭ to show your answer.

9. ⬭ wren
⬭ when
⬭ went

10. ⬭ sneak
⬭ kite
⬭ knock

© Pearson Education, Inc., 1

 Home Activity Your child read words that begin with *kn* as in *knight* and *wr* as in *wrench*. Have your child copy all the words from the page that begin with *kn* and *wr* and ask him or her to circle the silent letter in each word.

Name _____

Pick a word from the box to finish each compound word.
Write it on the line.
Draw a line to the picture it matches.

flashlight

boat   man   paper   watch

1. news _____

2. row _____

3. wrist _____

4. snow _____

Find the compound word.

Mark the ⬭ to show your answer.

5. ⬭ raining
   ⬭ rainy
   ⬭ raincoat

6. ⬭ popcorn
   ⬭ puppy
   ⬭ popping

7. ⬭ mitten
   ⬭ marching
   ⬭ backpack

8. ⬭ balloon
   ⬭ daydream
   ⬭ broken

© Pearson Education, Inc., 1

School + Home

Home Activity Your child read compound words—words formed by joining two or more words. Have your child tell what two words make up these compound words: *rainbow, snowflake, peanut, baseball, backpack.*

Name _____

Circle the word for each picture.

1.  blew black	**2.**  flow flew	**3.**  glue glow	**4.**  chick chew
5.  sit suit	**6.**  stew stop	**7.**  joke juice	**8.**  news nose

Read the words in the box.
Pick a word to finish each sentence.

    bruise   drew   true

9. It is _____ that I love ice cream.

10. He has a _____ on his leg.

11. My sister _____ this picture.

© Pearson Education, Inc., 1

 School + Home **Home Activity** Your child practiced reading words with *ew, ue,* and *ui* as in *blew, glue,* and *suit*. Work with your child to make up silly rhyming pairs that contain this vowel sound and these spellings, such as *blue stew* or *fruit suit*.

Name _____

Add -ly or -ful to the word in ( ).
Write the new word on the line.

nice + -ly = nice**ly**

(play)

_____

1. The dog is _____ .

(slow)

_____

2. The dog walked _____ .

(quick)

_____

3. Then it ran _____ !

(safe)

_____

4. The dog got home _____ .

(thank)

_____

5. Miss Moon was _____ .

School + Home **Home Activity** Your child added -ly and -ful to words. Ask your child to give you instructions using words with the -ly suffix, such as *Clap loudly; Talk softly; Walk quickly.* Follow the instructions. Then have your child write simple sentences using *playful* and *thankful.*

© Pearson Education, Inc., 1

71

Name _____

Circle the word for each picture.

1. 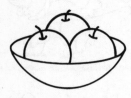	2. 	3. 	4. 
zoo zip	span spoon	pal pool	stool stale

5. 	6. 	7. 	8.
fruit fool	gaze goose	boot bait	spool spill

Pick a word to finish each sentence.

Write the word in the sentence.

9. The _____ blocked the cars on the road.

       moose   mouse

10. I dropped my _____ on the floor.

       farm   food

11. I used a _____ to clean up the mess.

       boot   broom

 Home Activity Your child practiced reading and creating words with *oo* as in *moon*. Write the *oo* words from this page on scraps of paper. Have your child pick a word and use it in a sentence.

© Pearson Education, Inc., 1

Name _____

Pick a word from the box to match each picture.
Write it on the line.

cr<u>ow</u>n

cloud	clown	flower	house

1. _____

2. _____

3. _____

4. _____

Unscramble the letters to make a word.

uodl _____   wtno _____   tuo _____

Pick a word to finish each sentence. **Write** it on the line.

5. The opposite of *in* is _____.

6. The radio was too _____.

7. I like to shop in _____.

Home Activity Your child read and wrote words with *ow* that have the vowel sound heard in *crown*.
Encourage your child to make a list of other words with *ow* that rhyme with *cow* and *brown*.

73

Name _____

Circle the word for each picture.

 bott**le**

1.	2.	3.	4.

cattle canned	tabbed table	picking pickle	turtle turned

5.	6.	7.	8.

candle candy	needy needle	handy handle	saddle sadder

Find the word that has the same ending sound as .
Mark the ⬭ to show your answer.

9. ⬭ litter
   ⬭ lightly
   ⬭ little

10. ⬭ purple
    ⬭ purred
    ⬭ purest

© Pearson Education, Inc., 1

School + Home **Home Activity** Your child read two-syllable words with -le in the second syllable. Have your child fold a sheet of paper into four boxes, choose four of the words he or she circled, find a rhyming word for that word, and draw pictures of the rhyming word. Ask your child to label each picture.

Name _____

Write a word from the box to match each picture.

| couch cow flour |
| snowman towel rowboat |

1.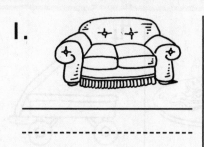

_____

_____

2.

_____

_____

3.

_____

_____

4.

_____

_____

5.

_____

_____

6.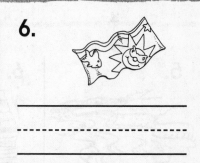

_____

_____

Write the word to finish each sentence. **Remember** to use capital letters at the beginning of a sentence.

_____

7. _____ does your garden grow? **how   have**

8. Can I come to play at your _____? **toy   house**

9. I like to _____ bubbles. **blue   blow**

10. I went _____ to take a walk. **outside   inside**

© Pearson Education, Inc., 1

Home Activity Your child read and wrote words with vowel patterns *ou* as in *couch*, and *ow* as in *cow* and *snow*. Encourage your child to make a list of words that rhyme with these vowel patterns.

75

Name _____

Circle the word for each picture.

 <u>so</u>fa

---

1.

lesson   lemon

2.

pillow   pilot

3.

bacon   basket

4.

wagging   wagon

5.

river   rigged

6.

cabin   cab

7.

timber   tiger

8.

came   camel

Draw a picture for each word.

9. spider

10. baby

© Pearson Education, Inc., 1

School + Home

Home Activity Your child read words with two syllables that have one consonant in the middle. Have your child choose five words from the page and use each word in a sentence.

Name _____

Circle the word for each picture.

1. 	2. 	3. 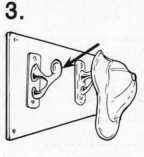	4. 
had hood	cook coat	hook hard	wide wood

5. 	6. 	7. 	8. 
bake book	look lock	store stood	brook brake

Read the words in the box.
Circle the words that have the same vowel sound as  .
Pick one of these words to finish each sentence.

> take   foot   took   soon   goat   tool   good

9. He _____ a picture of the lake.

10. That was a _____ joke.

11. My _____ hurts.

© Pearson Education, Inc., 1

Home Activity Your child read and wrote words with *oo* that have the vowel sound heard in *foot*. Encourage your child to make lists that sort the words into those that rhyme with *took* and those that rhyme with *good*.

Name _____

Add -s, -ed, or **-ing** to the word in ( ).
Write the new word on the line.

(hope + -s)

_____

1. Jean _____ to grow corn.

(slope + -ing)

_____

2. She plants seeds on the _____ hill.

(care + -ed)

_____

3. Jean _____ for the plants.

(taste + -ed)

_____

4. Jean _____ the corn.

(smile + -ing)

_____

5. She is _____ .

© Pearson Education, Inc, 1

School + Home

Home Activity Your child added -s, -ed, or -ing to verbs that end in e. Write hope, slope, care, taste, and smile on a sheet of paper. Ask your child to tell the rule about adding -s, -ed, or -ing to each word. Then write the new words.

Name _____

Circle the word for each picture.

 t**oy**    s**oi**l

1.	2.	3.	4.

coins canes	bay boy	boil bail	joy jay

5.	6.	7.	8.

boil book	all oil	foil fail	round royal

Pick a word to finish each sentence. **Write** the word in the sentence.

9. May I _____ you for lunch?   (jolly, join)

10. My favorite _____ is a racing car.   (tray, toy)

11. The meat will _____ in the hot sun.   (spoil, spool)

© Pearson Education, Inc., 1

 School + Home **Home Activity** Your child read and wrote words with *oi* and *oy* as heard in *toy* and *soil*. Have your child sort the *oi* and *oy* words on this page and make two lists. Then have him or her read the words aloud.

Name _____

Write a word from the box
to match each picture.

worker

baker   sailor   painter   teacher

1.

_____
- - - - - - - - - - - - - -

2.

_____
- - - - - - - - - - - - - -

3.

_____
- - - - - - - - - - - - - -

4.
_____
- - - - - - - - - - - - - -

Draw a picture of each word.

5. driver

6. actor

© Pearson Education, Inc., 1

School + Home

Home Activity Your child read and wrote words that end in *-er* and *-or* as in *worker* and *actor.* Write each word on a slip of paper. Have your child choose a slip and act out the word for you to guess.

Name _____

Circle the word for each picture.

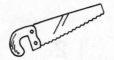 **saw**    **au**to

---

1.	2.	3.	4.

pail paw	yawn yard	lunch launch	stray straw

5.	6.	7.	8.
		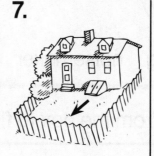	
false faucet	crawl call	lane lawn	laundry landed

Pick a word to finish each sentence. **Circle** the word.
Write the word in the sentence.

9. I like pasta with _____ .

sauce   sash

10. The bear used his _____ to open the bag.

clay   claw

© Pearson Education, Inc., 1

Home Activity Your child read words with the vowel sounds *aw* and *au* as heard in *saw* and *auto*. Have your child make silly rhyming sentences using words that rhyme with *saw*. Example: *The cat can draw with her paw*.

Name _____

Circle the word that names each picture.

1.

platter   painter   painting

2.

toyshop   trays   toolbox

3.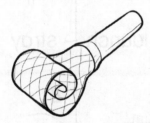

nose   nothing   noisemaker

4.

another   awning   author

Write the word from the box to finish each sentence.

| oatmeal   endpoint   football   boyhood |

5. A bowl of hot _____ is good for you.

6. I like to play _____.

7. He had a great _____.

8. A dot at the end of a line is an _____.

© Pearson Education, Inc., 1

School + Home **Home Activity** Your child read compound words with vowel diphthongs (*oi*, *oy*) and vowel digraphs (*oa*). Have your child read the following words aloud and then make up a sentence for each: *football*, *boyhood*, and *oatmeal*.

Name _____

Add re- or **un-** to the word in ( ).
Write the new word on the line.

re- + do = **re**do
un- + clear = **un**clear

(build)

_____

- -

1. Mr. Ford will _____ the car.

(happy)

_____

- -

2. He is _____ with the color.

(paint)

_____

- -

3. He will _____ it.

(fills)

_____

- -

4. He _____ the car with gas.

(lock)

_____

- -

5. Don't forget to _____ the door!

© Pearson Education, Inc., 1

School + Home

Home Activity Your child added the prefixes *un-* and *re-* to words. Ask your child to think of other words to which *un-* and *re-* can be added. Have him or her list the words and use them in sentences.

83

Name _____

Circle the word for each picture.

 p**ost**   g**old**    r**ind**    w**ild**

1. 	2. 	3. 	4. 
fold fell	kite kind	child chilled	mast most
5. 	6. 	7. 	8. 
cold call	fin find	wind went	old all

Circle the word to finish each sentence.

9. I told / tied my baby sister a story.

10. I can't fine / find my pencil.

© Pearson Education, Inc., 1

School + Home

Home Activity Your child read words with the long *o* sound as in *post* and *gold* and the long *i* sound as in *rind* and *wild*. Use each word in a sentence with your child.

84

Name _____

Read the words in the box.
Pick a word to finish each sentence.
Write it on the line.
Read the sentence from left to right.

> I   see   a   green

1. This is _____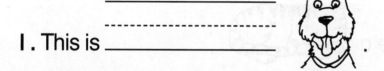

2. We _____ a _____ .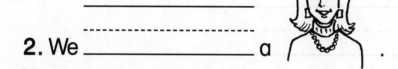

3. This is my _____ .

4. _____ am a _____ .

© Pearson Education, Inc., 1

Home Activity This week your child learned to identify and read the words *I*, *see*, *a*, and *green*. As you read with your child, encourage him or her to point out these words in print.

Name _____

Read the words in the box.
Pick a word to finish each sentence.
Write it on the line.
Read the sentence from left to right.

I   see   a   green

1. _____ have a _____ .

2. The _____ is _____ .

3. I _____ the _____ .

4. This is _____ .

© Pearson Education, Inc., 1

School + Home **Home Activity** This week your child identified and read the words *I, see, a,* and *green*. Write each word on a card. Have your child read each word and then use it in a sentence.

Name _____

Read the words in the box.
Pick a word to finish each sentence.
Write it on the line.

we	like	the	one

1. _____ see a 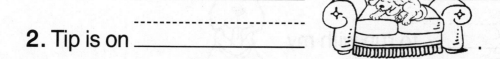 .

2. Tip is on _____ 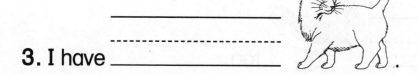 .

3. I have _____ .

4. I _____ our _____ .

© Pearson Education, Inc., 1

School + Home

Home Activity This week your child identified and read the words *we*, *like*, *the*, and *one*. As you read with your child, encourage him or her to point out these words in print.

Name _____

Read the words in the box.
Pick a word to finish each sentence.
Write it on the line.

> we   like   the   one

---

1. Here is _____ man.

---

2. I _____ to run with my  .

---

3. I have _____  too.

---

4. _____ have a and a  .

© Pearson Education, Inc., 1

School + Home

Home Activity This week your child identified and read the words *we, like, the,* and *one*. Write each word on a card. Have your child read each word and then use it in a sentence.

Name _____

Read the words in the box.
Pick a word to finish each sentence.
Write it on the line.

```
do    look    you    was    yellow
```

_____
- - - - - - - - - - - - - - - - - - -
1. Tip _____ sad.

_____
- - - - - - - - - - - - - - - - - - -
2. _____ in the  .

_____
- - - - - - - - - - - - - - - - - - -
3. _____ you see the  ?

_____
- - - - - - - - - - - - - - - - - - -
4. The  is _____ .

_____
- - - - - - - - - - - - - - - - - - -
5. _____ can hold the  .

© Pearson Education, Inc., 1

Home Activity This week your child identified and read the words *do, look, you, was,* and *yellow*. As you read with your child, encourage him or her to point out these words in print.

89

Name _____

Read the words in the box.
Pick a word to finish each sentence.
Write it on the line.

| do   look   you   was   yellow |

1. This  is _____ .
   _____

2. _____ Can _____ see the  ?

3. _____ _____ at that big  !

4. The  _____ in the bag!

5. _____ you like my _____ ?

School + Home

Home Activity This week your child learned to read the words *do, look, you, was,* and *yellow*. Write each word on a card. Have your child read each word and then use it in a sentence.

© Pearson Education, Inc., 1

Name _____

Read the words in the box.
Pick a word to finish each sentence.
Write it on the line. **Remember** to begin a sentence with a capital letter.

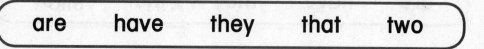

are	have	they	that	two

1. _____ are playing in the _____ .

2. Look at _____ white _____ .

3. We _____ a little _____ .

4. My _____ went home.

5. There _____ three _____ .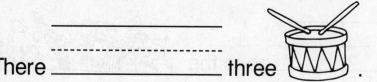

© Pearson Education, Inc., 1

 School + Home

Home Activity This week your child identified and read the words *are, have, they, that,* and *two.* As you read with your child, encourage him or her to point out these words in print.

91

Name _____

Read the words in the box.
Pick a word to finish each sentence.
Write it on the line.

> are   have   they   that   two

1. I like _____ pretty _____ .

2. The _____ all black.

3. Stella has _____ big _____ .

4. Jan and Pete _____ funny _____ .

5. When will _____ go to the  ?

© Pearson Education, Inc., 1

School + Home

Home Activity This week your child identified and read the words *are, have, they, that,* and *two*. As you read with your child, encourage him or her to point out these words in print.

Name _____

Read the words in the box.
Pick a word to finish each sentence.
Write it on the line. **Remember** to begin each sentence with a capital letter.

> he   is   to   with   three

---

1. She _____ on the  .

---

2. Bill came _____  .

---

3. We have _____ books.

---

4. My  are _____ me.

---

5. _____ has a cat.

© Pearson Education, Inc., 1

Home Activity This week your child identified and read the words *he, is, to, with,* and *three.* As you read with your child, encourage him or her to point out these words in print.

Name _____

Read the words in the box.
Pick a word to finish each sentence.
Write it on the line.

| he | is | to | with | three |

1. Basketball _____ fun.
   _____

2. The _____ squirrels are eating .
   _____

3. Sam likes to play _____ Pat.
   _____

4. We can go _____ the party Saturday.
   _____

5. When will _____ move to his new house?
   _____

© Pearson Education, Inc., 1

School + Home

Home Activity This week your child identified and read the words *he, is, to, with,* and *three.* As you read with your child, encourage him or her to point out these words in print.

94

Name _____

Read the words in the box.
Pick a word to finish each sentence. **Write** it on the line.
Remember to begin a sentence with a capital letter.

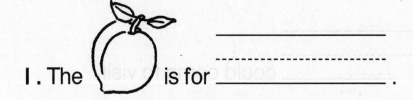

where   he   for   me   go

1. The is for _____ .

2. We are waiting _____ the rain to stop.

3. _____ can we buy pickles?

4. Let's _____ to the Farmers Market.

5. _____ had three yams.

© Pearson Education, Inc., 1

School + Home
Home Activity This week your child identified and read the words *where, he, for, me,* and *go.* As you read with your child, encourage him or her to point out these words in print.

Name _____

Read the words in the box.
Pick a word to finish each sentence.
Write it on the line.

> where   he   for   me   go

1. Viv asked Tim if _____ could come to visit.

2. The rainbow may _____ away.

3. I know _____ you live.

4. Bill can come with _____ to the game.

5. She bought vegetables _____ Jan.

Home Activity This week your child identified and read the words *where, he, for, me,* and *go*. As you read with your child, encourage him or her to point out these words in print.

© Pearson Education, Inc., 1

Name _____

Read the words in the box.
Pick a word to finish each sentence.
Write it on the line.

> my   on   way   in   come

1. We go that _____ to the  .
   ----

2. The can _____ to me.

3. This is _____  .

4. The is _____ my  .

5. The is _____ my .

© Pearson Education, Inc., 1

School + Home

Home Activity This week your child identified and read the words *in, on, my, way,* and *come*. Write each word on a card. Have your child read each word and then use it in a sentence.

Name _____

Read the words in the box. **Pick** a word to finish each sentence.
Write it on the line. **Remember** to use a capital
letter at the beginning of a sentence.

| up   take   she   what |

_____
- -
1. My cat is _____ .

_____
- -
2. You can _____ two.

_____
- -
3. _____ has a pack.

_____
- -
4. _____ can Nan fix?

© Pearson Education, Inc., 1

School + Home

Home Activity This week your child identified and read the words *up, take, she,* and *what.* As you read with
your child, encourage him or her to point out these words in print.

98

Name _____

Read the words in the box.
Pick a word to finish each sentence.
Write it on the line.

blue	from	help	little	get	use

_____

1. Can I _____ your ?

_____

2. I can take it _____ you.

_____

3. I will _____ a  .

_____

4. My dogs _____ you go.

_____

5. I see a big _____ ox!

_____

6. The dogs are _____ .

© Pearson Education, Inc., 1

Home Activity This week your child identified and read the words *get, blue, from, help, little,* and *use.* Encourage your child to find these words in everyday print.

Name _____

Read the words in the box.
Pick a word to finish each sentence.
Write it on the line. **Remember** to begin a sentence with a capital letter.

> eat   four   five   her   this   too

1. We see _____

   _____ 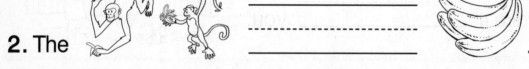 .

2. The _____

   _____ 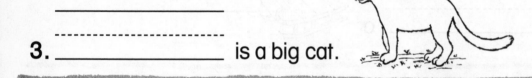 .

3. _____

   _____ is a big cat.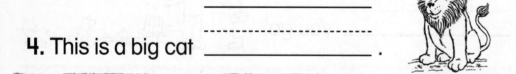

4. This is a big cat _____

   _____ .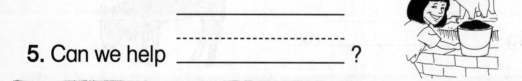

5. Can we help _____

   _____ ?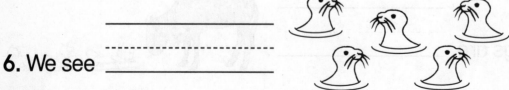

6. We see _____

   _____ .

© Pearson Education, Inc., 1

School + Home

Home Activity This week your child identified and read the words *eat, four, five, her, too,* and *this.* Look through books to find these words in print and have your child read them aloud.

100

Name _____

Read the words in the box.
Pick a word to finish each sentence.
Write it on the line. **Remember** to use a capital letter at the beginning of a sentence.

| saw   small   tree   your |

1. We _____ a tree.

2. It was not a big _____.

3. Do you like this _____ tree?

4. _____ tree is not wet.

Home Activity This week your child identified and read the words *saw, small, tree,* and *your.* Make flashcards with one word on each card. Mix them up and have your child read the words.

© Pearson Education, Inc., 1

Name _____

Read the words in the box.
Pick a word to finish each sentence.
Write it on the line.

home   into   many   them

1. This is a _____ for 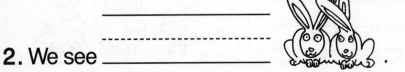 .

2. We see _____ 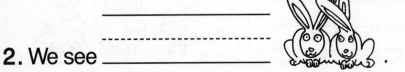 .

3. Do you see _____ ?

4. The 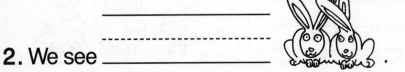 go _____ the home.

Draw a picture of you going into your home.

5.

© Pearson Education, Inc., 1

Home Activity Your child identified and read the words *home, into, many,* and *them.* Invite your child to use the words to describe life in his or her home.

Name _____

Read the words in the box.
Pick a word from the box to finish each sentence.
Write it on the line.

catch	good	no	put	said	want

_____
- -
1. Dad and Bob _____ to fish.

_____
- -
2. "You can _____ it here," Dad said.

_____
- -
3. "I will," _____ Bob.

_____
- -
4. Bob has _____ fish yet.

_____
- -
5. Bob can _____ that fish!

_____
- -
6. It is a _____ fish.

© Pearson Education, Inc., 1

School + Home

Home Activity Your child identified and read the words *catch, good, no, put, said,* and *want.* As you read with your child, encourage him or her to point out these words in print.

Name _____

Read the words in the box.
Pick a word to finish each sentence.
Write it on the line.

| be | could | horse | of | old | paper |

1. Dad gave me a _____ .

2. She was not _____ .

3. She _____ run and jump.

4. I put her name on a _____ .

5. I can make the horse the color _____ a fox.

6. We will _____ pals!

Home Activity Your child identified and read the words *be, of, could, horse, old,* and *paper*. Write these words on small pieces of paper or self-stick notes. Tape them on a mirror or desk for your child to practice every day.

© Pearson Education, Inc., 1

Name _____

Read the words in the box.
Pick a word to finish each sentence.
Write it on the line. **Remember** to use capital letters at the beginning of a sentence.

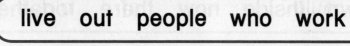

live   out   people   who   work

1. _____ can fix this clock?

2. The _____ in the shop can fix it.

3. They will _____ on it.

4. Where does your dog _____ ?

5. His home is _____ here.

© Pearson Education, Inc., 1

School + Home

Home Activity Your child identified and read the words *live, out, people, who,* and *work.* Point to these words on the page. Have your child read each word and use it in a spoken sentence.

Name _____

Read the words in the box.
Pick a word from the box to match each clue.
Write it on the line.

> down   inside   now   there   together

1. not up

_____

- - - - - - - - - - - - -

_____

2. not here

_____

- - - - - - - - - - - - -

_____

3. not outside

_____

- - - - - - - - - - - - -

_____

4. not then

_____

- - - - - - - - - - - - -

_____

5. not one here and not one there

_____

- - - - - - - - - - - - -

_____

© Pearson Education, Inc., 1

School + Home

Home Activity Your child identified and read the words *down, inside, now, there,* and *together.* Read one word aloud. Have your child point to it and use it in a sentence. Repeat with the other words.

Name _____

Look at each picture.
Read the words.
Write the word on the line that best fits the picture.

1.

find
around

_____

2.

water
food

_____

3.

around
under

_____

4.

grow
find

_____

5.

water
under

_____

6.

food
water

_____

© Pearson Education, Inc., 1

School + Home **Home Activity** Your child identified and read the words *around*, *find*, *food*, *grow*, *under*, and *water*. Make up clues for the words on this page. Ask your child to identify the words. Challenge your child to think of some clues too.

Name _____

Read the words in the box.
Pick a word from the box to match each clue.
Write the words in the puzzles.

| also   family   new   other   some   their |

1. not a lot

2. too

3.

4. not old

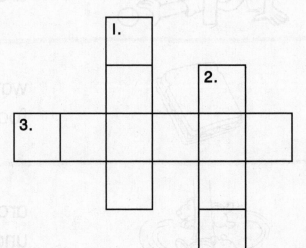

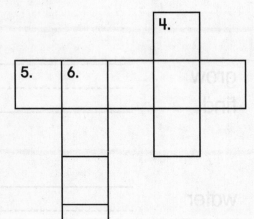

5. It's not this one. It's the
   _____ one.

6. It's not my food.
   It's _____ food.

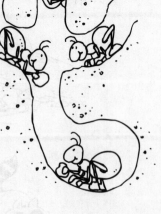

© Pearson Education, Inc., 1

School + Home
Home Activity Your child identified and read the words *also, family, new, other, some,* and *their.* Help your child to make up a story or poem using these words. Work together to write the story or poem and read it to other family members.

Name _____

Read the words in the box. **Pick** a word to finish each sentence.
Write it on the line.

> always becomes day everything
> nothing stays things

1. Jazzy likes to play all _____ .

2. _____ can stop him!

3. He gets into _____ .

4. He _____ makes a mess.

5. Jazzy _____ in my room.

6. He hides _____ under the bed.

7. He rests when he _____ sleepy.

© Pearson Education, Inc., 1

Home Activity This week your child identified and read the words *always*, *becomes*, *day*, *everything*, *nothing*, *stays*, and *things*. Use paper bag puppets to act out a scene using these new words.

Name _____

Read the words in the box.
Write a word to finish each sentence.

any	enough	ever
every	own	sure	were

1. Do we have ☐☐☐☐☐☐ food?

2. Yes, I am ☐☐☐ we do.

3. Is ☐☐☐☐ place set?

4. Yes, they ☐☐☐ set last night.

5. Do you need ☐☐☐ flowers?

6. No, I have my ☐☐☐ .

7. This will be the best day ☐☐☐ !

© Pearson Education, Inc., 1

Home Activity This week your child identified and read the words *any, enough, ever, every, own, sure,* and *were*. Help your child make up a short story using some of these words. Then help your child to write down the sentences and draw a picture to go with his or her story.

110

Name _____

Read the words in the box.
Pick a word to finish each sentence.
Write it on the line.

> away car friends house our school very

1. This is our new _____ .

2. It is by my _____ .

3. It is _____ nice.

4. We go with our _____ .

5. They come in a _____ .

6. My mom will walk _____ . I will stay.

7. _____ teacher is inside.

School + Home

Home Activity This week your child identified and read the words *away, car, friends, house, our, school,* and *very*. Use sock puppets to act out a new story using the words. Help your child write down the story you create.

111

Name _____

Circle a word to finish each sentence.
Write it on the line.

how   few

_____

1. We have a _____ 📖 to take back.

---

afraid   read

_____

2. We _____ them all and came for new ones.

again   few

_____

3. Can we get some _____ ?

---

soon   how

_____

4. We can read _____ to plant flowers.

---

afraid   few

_____

5. I am _____ this is not the best one.

---

afraid   soon

_____

6. My mom will be here _____ .

School + Home

Home Activity This week your child identified and read the words *afraid*, *again*, *few*, *how*, *read*, and *soon*.
Make some flash cards and have your child practice reading the words.

© Pearson Education, Inc., 1

Name _____

Read the words in the box.
Pick a word to finish each sentence.
Write the words in the puzzles.

| push   visit   wait |

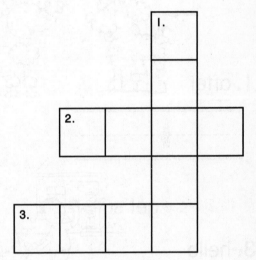

1. We'll _____ our
   friends soon.

2. They will _____ us
   on the swings.

3. I can not _____ !

| done   know |

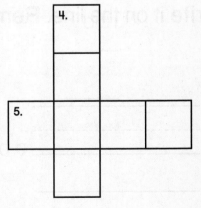

4. I _____ we will do well!

5. We will try to win.
   We will be happy
   when we are _____ .

© Pearson Education, Inc., 1

Home Activity Your child identified and read the words *done, know, push, visit,* and *wait.* Write the words on a sheet of paper. Give your child a clue for each word. Then have him or her guess the word and point to it.

Name _____

Read the words in the box.
Pick a word that is the opposite of each word below.
Write it on the line.

before   good-bye   right   won't

1. after _____

2. will _____

3. hello _____

4. wrong _____

$$\begin{array}{r} 2 \\ +2 \\ \hline 4 \end{array}$$

Pick a word from the box to finish each sentence.
Write it on the line. **Remember** to use capital letters.

oh   does

5. _____ a bear start its long sleep in the spring?

6. _____ , no. It sleeps when the days start to get cold.

Home Activity Your child identified and read the words *before, good-bye, right,* and *won't*. Write the opposite of these words on cards and mix them up. Have your child match the words that are opposites and then read the pairs. Then have him or her write two sentences using *does* and *oh*.

114

© Pearson Education, Inc., 1

Name _____

Read the words in the box.
Pick a word to complete each sentence.
Look at the scrambled letters for a hint.
Write the word on the line.

about   enjoy   gives   surprise
surprised   worry   would

1. I _____ helping. **nyjeo**

2. We eat at _____ 12:00. **buato**

3. _____ you please help me? **odluw**

4. Do not _____ . I will help. **woryr**

5. When we jump up, she will be _____ . **sipresrud**

6. Dad _____ us gifts. **ivseg**

7. The gifts are always a big _____ . **rrpsiues**

© Pearson Education, Inc., 1

School + Home **Home Activity** Your child identified and read the words *about, enjoy, gives, surprise, surprised, worry,* and *would*. Ask your child to use these words to create a puppet show with paper bag puppets. Record the script on paper and have your child practice reading it aloud.

Name _____

Read the words in the box.
Pick a word to complete each sentence.
Write the word on the line.

> draw   colors   over
> drew   great   sign   show

1. Each day I like to _____ in art class.

2. Ted did a _____ job on his drawing!

3. I can read the _____ on the gate.

4. I think red and blue are the best _____ .

5. The map will _____ us the way to go.

6. The frogs jump _____ the rocks.

7. Last week I _____ a dog in art class.

School + Home

Home Activity Your child identified and read the words *draw, colors, over, drew, great, sign,* and *show.*
Have your child read each word again and make up a new sentence for each word.

116

Name _____

Read the words in the box.
Pick a word to finish each sentence.
Write it in the puzzle.

> found   mouth   once   took   wild

1. You talk with your _____ .

2. "_____ upon a time . . ."

3. not lost

4. He _____ three bites
of his cake.

5. A raccoon is a _____ animal.

© Pearson Education, Inc., 1

 Home Activity Your child identified and read the words *found*, *mouth*, *once*, *took*, and *wild*. Ask your child to write and illustrate a fairy tale about a boy or girl who finds a wild animal. Encourage your child to use the new words and help him or her with spelling if necessary.

117

Name _____

Read the words in the box.
Pick a word to match each clue.
Write it on the line.

> above   eight   laugh   moon   touch

1.  "Ha, ha, ha!" _____

2. **8** five, six, seven, _____

3. 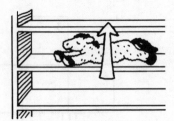 not below _____

4.  feel _____

5. stars, planets, _____

© Pearson Education, Inc., 1

Home Activity Your child identified and read the words *above, eight, laugh, moon,* and *touch*. Act out clues for each word and have your child guess which word you picked.

118

Name _____

Read the words in the box.
Pick a word to finish each sentence.
Write it on the line.

picture   remember   room   stood   thought   would

_____
- -
1. Mom took a _____ of my friends and me.

_____
- -
2. We _____ by a tree.

_____
- -
3. I _____ the picture was wonderful.

_____
- -
4. I will hang the picture in my _____ .

_____
- -
5. It will help me _____ my friends.

© Pearson Education, Inc., 1

School + Home **Home Activity** Your child learned to identify and read the words *picture, remember, room, stood,* and *thought.* Write each word on a small piece of paper. Say each word. Have your child put the words in the order in which you read them and then repeat the words in a different order.

Name _____

Read the words in the box.
Pick a word to match each clue.
Write it on the line.

> across   because   dance   only   opened   shoes   told

1.

_____

_ _ _ _ _ _ _ _ _ _ _ _ _ _ _ _ _ _

2.

_____

_ _ _ _ _ _ _ _ _ _ _ _ _ _ _ _ _ _

3.

_____

_ _ _ _ _ _ _ _ _ _ _ _ _ _ _ _ _ _

4. She said, "I _____ you to read slowly."

_____

_ _ _ _ _ _ _ _ _ _ _ _ _ _ _ _ _ _

5. The plant grows _____ it has water.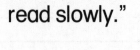

_____

_ _ _ _ _ _ _ _ _ _ _ _ _ _ _ _ _ _

6. Mom said, "_____ one treat!"

_____

_ _ _ _ _ _ _ _ _ _ _ _ _ _ _ _ _ _

© Pearson Education, Inc., 1

7.

_____

_ _ _ _ _ _ _ _ _ _ _ _ _ _ _ _ _ _

 School + Home

Home Activity Your child learned to read the words *across, because, dance, only, opened, shoes,* and *told.* Make up more clues for the words on this page. Ask your child to identify the words. Challenge your child to think of some clues.

120

Name _____

Read the words in the box.
Pick a word to finish each sentence. **Write** it on the line.
Remember to use a capital letter at the beginning of a sentence.

> along   behind   eyes   never   pulling   toward

1. The dogs walked _____ the wall.

2. The dogs stopped _____ the puddle.

3. Mom is _____ the boy away.

4. _____ pet a dog you do not know well.

5. The puppy ran _____ its mother.

6. Its _____ were happy and bright.

Home Activity Your child learned to identify and read the words *along*, *behind*, *eyes*, *never*, *pulling*, and *toward*. Ask your child to make up a puppet show using this week's words. Write out the script that your child dictates. Use paper bags or stick puppets to act it out.

© Pearson Education, Inc., 1

Name _____

Read the words in the box.
Pick a word to finish each sentence.
Write it on the line.

```
door   loved   should   wood
```

Dear Jack,

I had such a good time at your house last week.

I _____ it when we played in the snow!
Remember when we made an igloo?

We used a blanket for the _____, and it froze stiff.

You _____ come to my house!
It is very warm here even in the winter.

My dad and I are going to paint the _____ rail.

Your friend,

Sam

© Pearson Education, Inc., 1

Home Activity Your child learned to identify and read the words *door, loved, should,* and *wood.* Ask your child to write a story that uses each word and read it aloud.

Name _____

Read the sentence. **Unscramble** the letters.
Write the word on the line. **Remember** to use
a capital letter at the beginning of a sentence.

> among   another   instead   none

1. I will have **ahernot**.

   _____
   -
   _____

2. **eNon** of the fruit is left.

   _____
   -
   _____

3. Eat this **ineadst**.

   _____
   -
   _____

4. He likes to nap **angmo** his dogs.

   _____
   -
   _____

Home Activity Your child learned to identify and read the words *among, another, instead,* and *none.* Write
sentences such as these: *Is there another towel like this one? Try this one instead. None of the pie is left.*
Leave a blank where the word should be, and have your child fill it in.

© Pearson Education, Inc., 1

123

Name _____

Read the words in the box.
Pick a word to finish each sentence.
Write it in the puzzle.

against   goes   heavy   kinds   today

1. We push the
   umbrella _____ the wind.

2. The rain _____ into
   our shoes.

3. We play all _____ of
   games in the big puddles!

4. Rain this _____ does
   not happen often.

5. We will need
   dry socks _____ !

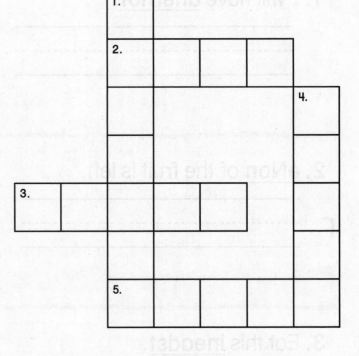

© Pearson Education, Inc., 1

School + Home

Home Activity Your child learned to read the words *against*, *goes*, *heavy*, *kinds*, and *today*. Ask your child to use the words in a silly song. Write the words of the song and invite him or her to illustrate it.

Name _____

Read the sentence.
Unscramble the letters.
Write the word on the line.

| built   early   learn   science   through |

_____
- -
1. Many boys and girls like **sciceen**. _____

_____
- - - - - - - - - - - - - - - - - - -
2. We **lnear** about plants. _____

3. We get up **earyl** to see the
_____
- - - - - - - - - - - - - - - - - - -
sun rise. _____

_____
- - - - - - - - - - - - - - - - - - -
4. We **uiltb** a little car! _____

_____
- - - - - - - - - - - - - - - - - - -
5. We look **ourghth** the glass. _____

Home Activity Your child learned to identify and read the words *built, early, learn, science,* and *through.* Find children's books about famous scientists and mathematicians. Read them together and challenge your child to find the words in the text.

© Pearson Education, Inc., 1

Name _____

Pick a word from the box to finish each sentence.
Write it on the line.

> poor answered
> different carry

1. The soil was so _____ that nothing grew.

2. I _____ all the questions about my garden.

3. All of the flowers were _____ colors.

4. I have to _____ the garden tools to the backyard.

Pick two words from the box.
Write your own sentences using each word.

5. _____

6. _____

7. _____

8. _____

© Pearson Education, Inc., 1

School + Home

Home Activity Your child learned to read and identify the words *answered, carry, different,* and *poor.*
Encourage your child to make up a story that uses these words and draw pictures to illustrate the story.

Name _____

Jack and Dad Pack

Short a		Final –ck	High-Frequency Words
at	cap ran	Jack	I
bag	Dad sat	back	said
and	had van	sack	the
bat	hat	pack	look
can	map		

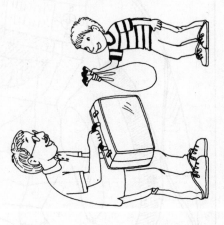

Jack and Dad sat.

"I can pack the bag," said Dad.

"I can pack the sack," said Jack.

© Pearson Education, Inc., 1

Dad had the bag at the van.

Jack ran back!

4

Decodable Story *Jack and Dad Pack*
Target Skill Short a, Final –ck

127

"I can pack the map," said Dad.
"I can pack the hat."

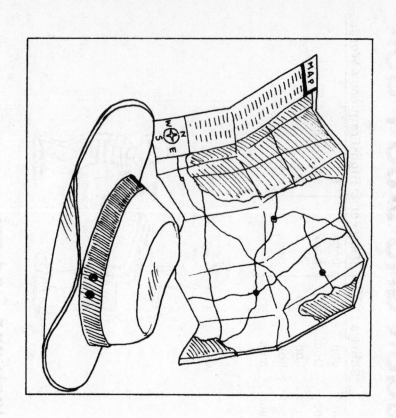

"I can pack the bat and cap," said Jack.
"Look at the sack!" said Dad.

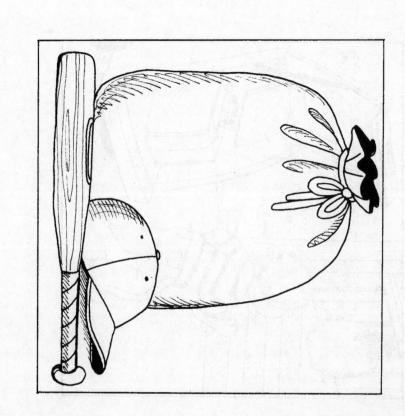

© Pearson Education, Inc., 1

Name _____

Jill Can!

Short i			Consonant x /ks/	High-Frequency Words
pick	zip	fit	six	is
quick	pin	sit	fix	the
Jill	rip	win		with
will	lid			

Jill is six.

Jill can zip.

Jill can pin the rip.

© Pearson Education, Inc., 1

Jill can pick the bat.

Jill is quick!

Jill will win.

Decodable Story *Jill Can!*
Target Skill Short *i*, Consonant *x/ks/*

Jill can fix the lid.
The lid will fit.

© Pearson Education, Inc., 1

Jill can pat the cat.
The cat will sit with Jill.

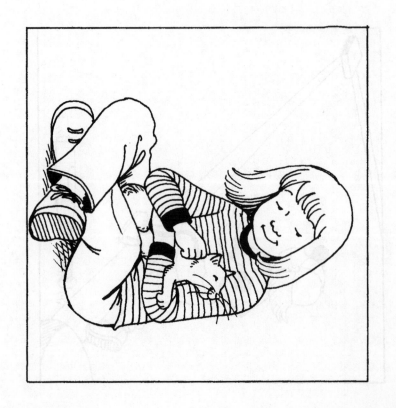

Name _____

What Is In the Box?

Short o		Plural -s + Consonant s/z/	High-Frequency Words	
box	not	rocks	are	go
fox	on	socks	in	is
got	top	**mops**	the	what
Dot				

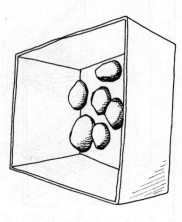

Are rocks in the box?

Six rocks are in the box.

© Pearson Education, Inc., 1

A fox is not in the box.

The fox is on top!

Decodable Story *What Is In the Box?*
Target Skills Skills Short *o*, Plural *-s* + Consonant *s/z/*

131

Are mops in the box?
The mops are in the box.

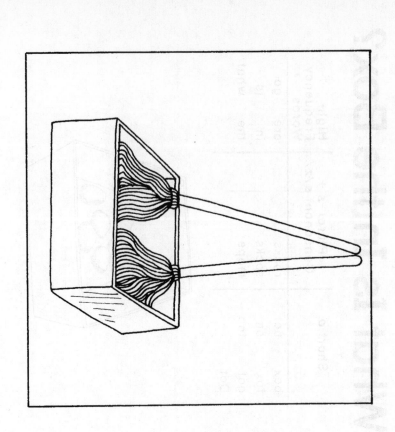

© Pearson Education, Inc., 1

Dot got the socks.
The socks can go in the box.

Rob

Inflected ending -s	Inflected ending -ing	High-Frequency Words	
fills	mixing	do	the
digs	tossing	of	up
picks	fixing	is	too
sits			

Rob will do lots of jobs.

Mom is mixing in the pot.

Rob fills the pan.

2

© Pearson Education, Inc., 1

Kit sits and sips.

Rob mops up.

Kit naps. Rob naps, too!

4

Dad digs the rocks.

Rob is tossing the rocks in the box.

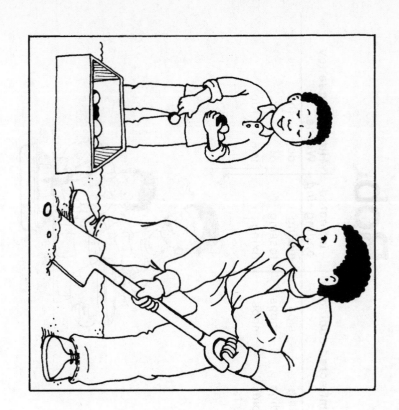

© Pearson Education, Inc., 1

Tam is fixing the rip in the cap.

Rob picks up the pins.

Name _____

The Blocks

Short e		Initial consonant blends	High Frequency Words
Meg	bed	blocks	the
gets	fell	black	a
ten	Peg	step	up
red	mess	stack	help
sets	yells		

Meg gets ten blocks.

Meg has red blocks.

Meg has black blocks.

© Pearson Education, Inc., 1

"Pick up the blocks," Mom yells.

"Peg will help!"

4

Meg sets the blocks on the step.
Meg will stack the blocks on the bed.

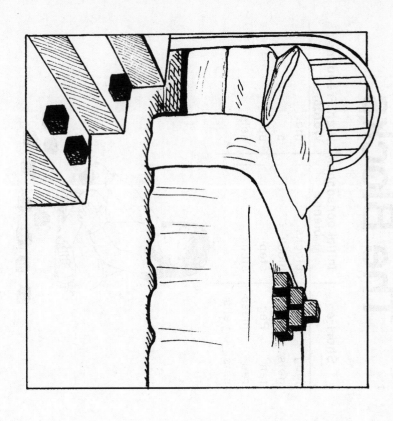

The blocks fell.
Peg got Mom.
"Meg has a mess!"

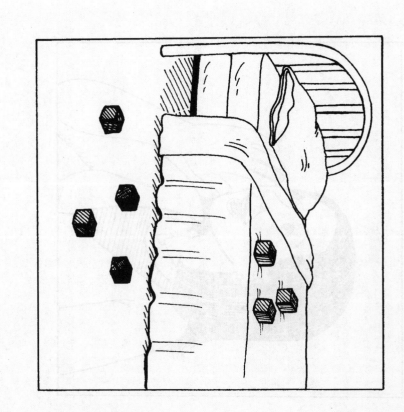

© Pearson Education, Inc., 1

Name _____

The Test

Short u		Final Consonant Blends	High-Frequency Words	
Huff	fun	test	must	the	said
Bud	stuck	best		a	is
sum	sums				

"The class will get a test," said
Miss Huff.

"The class will add."

© Pearson Education, Inc., 1

Bud got the sums.

Bud did his best.

Bud did well!

4

Decodable Story The Test
Target Skills Short *u*, Final Consonant Blends

137

1 + 1. Bud gets the sum.

3 + 3. The sum is six.

The test is fun!

© Pearson Education, Inc., 1

5 + 5. Bud is stuck.

Bud must get the sum.

The sum is ten.

Name

Cans

Consonant Digraphs	Vowel Sound in *ball and walk*	High-Frequency Words
shed	all	she
cash	walk	the
Smith	talks	to
with		do
then		
trash		
crush		
smash		

Miss Smith has cans.

She will not fill the trash with cans.

© Pearson Education, Inc., 1

Miss Smith talks with Ned.

"Do not fill the land with trash!"

4

Miss Smith will walk to the shed.
She will crush and smash the cans.

2

Miss Smith will fill all the bins with cans.
Then she will get cash.

© Pearson Education, Inc., 1

3

Jake takes the fast lane.

See Jake dash past the gate.

Jake is fast for his age!

The Race

Long *a*: *a_e*			Consonants *c /s/* and *g /j/*	High-Frequency Words	
Jake	gate	lane	race	I	see
lake	late	shape	pace	the	is
cake	skates	shade	place	of	for
takes	waves		age		
ate	came		Page		

Jake waves at Page. "I am in shape!"

"I will win the race at the lake."

© Pearson Education, Inc., 1

Page waves at Jake.

"I came late. I ate lots of cake.

I will get last place."

2

Page walks in the shade.

She is not fast.

"I wish I had skates!"

© Pearson Education, Inc., 1

3

© Pearson Education, Inc., 1

Name _____

The White Kite

Long i: i_e		Consonant Digraphs wh, ch, tch, ph	High-Frequency Words
kite	nice	white	the
quite	line	checks	I
mile	dives	patch	a
smiles	like	Ralph	is
			go

Ralph calls Ann on the cell.

"I made a white kite!"

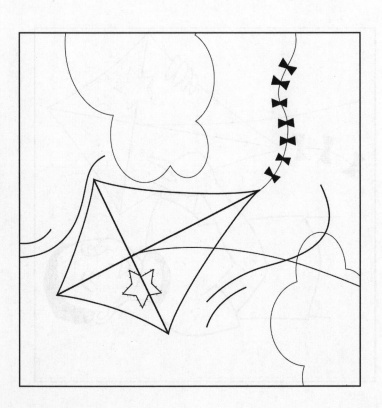

Ralph lets the kite go up.

It dips and dives.

"I like this kite!" Ralph tells Ann.

4

Ann checks the kite.

"It is small. But it is quite nice!"

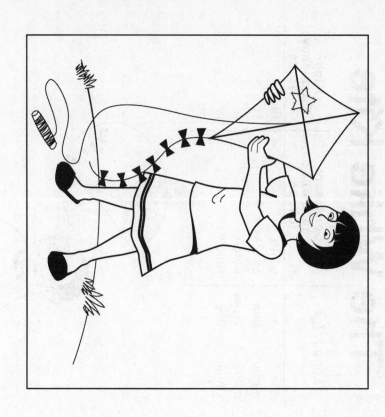

Ralph smiles.

"The kite has a patch and a line.

It will go up a mile!"

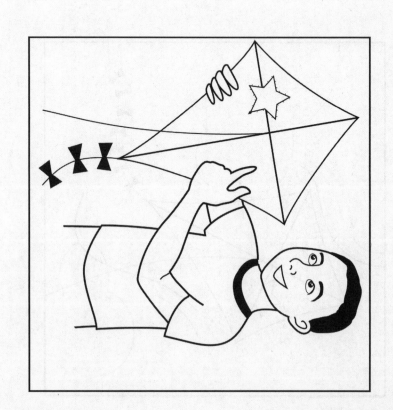

© Pearson Education, Inc., 1

Name _____

© Pearson Education, Inc., 1

What Am I?

Long o: o_e		Contractions n't, 'm, 'll		High-Frequency Words
nose	rope	I'm	can't	a	what
hole	pole	you'll	isn't	I	me
bone	globe			see	

I'm on a face.

I can't see, but I can smell.

What am I? (I'm a nose!)

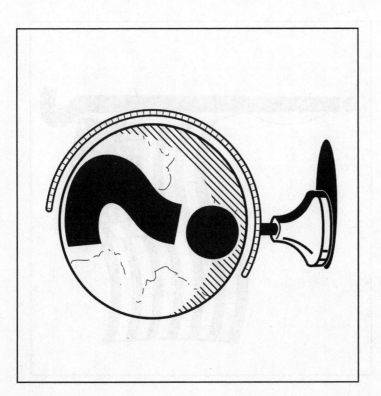

I'm a ball that isn't in a game.

You'll see shapes and lines on me.

What am I? (I'm a globe!)

4

Decodable Story *What Am I?*
Target Skill Long *o: o_e*, Contractions *n't, 'm, 'll*

145

You'll put me in the trash.
A pup puts me in a hole.
What am I? (I'm a bone!)

I'm tall and thin.
You'll see a flag and rope on me.
What am I? (I'm a pole!)

© Pearson Education, Inc., 1

Name _____

Duke the Mule

Long u / Long e		Inflected Ending –ed		High-Frequency Words	
Pete	mule	yelled	jumped	a	he
cute	cube	handed	helped	is	was
Duke				the	now

Pete has a cute pet.

His pet is Duke the mule.

© Pearson Education, Inc., 1

In June the gate broke.

Duke handed Pete a wire.

Duke helped fix the gate!

4

Duke had a trick when he was small.

Pete yelled "Jump!"

Then Duke jumped past the cube.

Now Duke is big.

He walks places. He takes naps.

But Duke still has tricks.

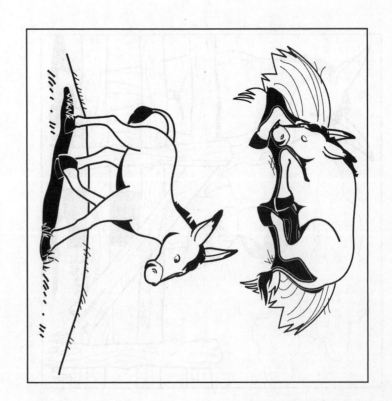

© Pearson Education, Inc., 1

© Pearson Education, Inc., 1

Name _____

Seeds

Long e: e, ee		VC/CV words	High-Frequency Words
he	needed	happen	to
be	weeds	problems	the
Lee	keep	insects	for
beet	weeks	basket	what
beets	see		watered
seeds	we'll		

Lee had seeds.

He needed to plant the seeds.

"What will the seeds be?" he asked.

Lee picked beets in six weeks.

"See the basket?" asked Lee.

"We'll get beets for lunch!"

4

Lee had problems.

Weeds came in.

Lee had to keep insects off.

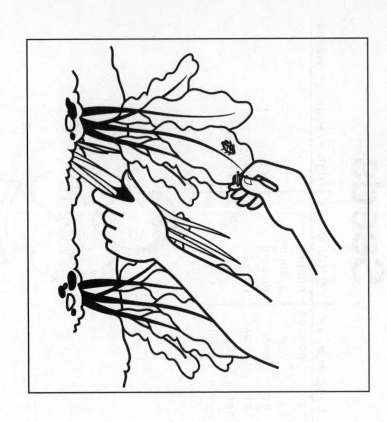

Lee dug holes for the seeds.

He watered the seeds.

"What will happen?" he asked.

© Pearson Education, Inc., 1

© Pearson Education, Inc., 1

Name _____

I'll Try It!

Vowel sounds of y:		Syllable Pattern CV		High-Frequency Words
my	bumpy	hi	hello	said
try	Katy	tiny	Bo	the
Jody	picky	we	no	is
funny	Molly	me		to
mushy	fluffy	be		
yucky	yummy	so		

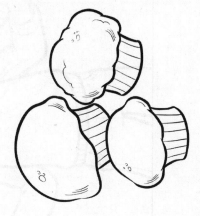

"Hi!" said Jody.

"Hello!" said the kids.

"We got muffins at the shop."

"Try my muffin," said Molly.

"It is fluffy and yummy."

"No," said Jody. "It is tiny!"

"My muffin tastes funny.

It is so mushy," said Bo.

"Hand it to me. I'll try it!" Jody yelled.

© Pearson Education, Inc., 1

"My muffin is yucky.

It is bumpy," said Katy.

"Don't be so picky," Jody said. "I'll try it!"

© Pearson Education, Inc., 1

Name _____

The King Sings a Song

Consonant Patterns *ng* and *nk*		Compound Words		High-Frequency Words	
think	king	upset	anything	a	do
pink	sing	inside	baseball	I	said
thanks	song	himself	hilltop	of	the
honk	long	cannot	rosebuds	to	

A king felt upset.

He sat inside by himself.

"I cannot think of anything to do," he said.

"I will sing with them," said the king.

"I will sing a long song.

Then I will be happy!"

4

"Get the baseball," said the queen.

"We can toss it on the hilltop."

"No, thanks," said the king.

"Take a walk," said the princess.

"See the rosebuds. Pet the pink pigs.

The geese will honk a song."

© Pearson Education, Inc., 1

Name _____

Six Wishes

Ending -*es* and plural -*es*		*r*-controlled *or* and *ore*		High-Frequency Words	
fetches	foxes	porch	chores	a	said
hatches	buses	for	snored	the	of
wishes	boxes	horn	snores	I	is
		more			

Elf sat on the porch.

"I will grant six wishes," said Elf.

"This will be fun," said the foxes.

© Pearson Education, Inc., 1

Funny Fox snored. Elf got a horn.

"I will grant this last wish.

No more snores!" said Elf.

Decodable Story *Six Wishes*
Target Skills Endings -*es*; Plural -*es*; *r*-controlled *or*, *ore*

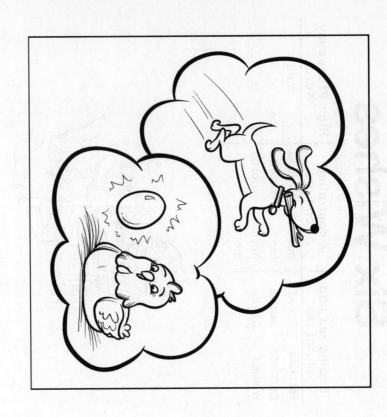

Franny Fox wished for a pet that fetches.

"Can I get a hen that hatches fancy eggs?" asked Freddy Fox.

© Pearson Education, Inc., 1

Sleepy Fox wished for buses.

Winky Fox wished for boxes of dishes.

"My wish is no more chores," said Franky Fox.

© Pearson Education, Inc., 1

Name _____

The Cart

Adding endings-double final consonants		r-controlled *ar*		High-Frequency Words	
humming	grabbed	Arty	started	a	said
running	stepped	cart	Marny	I	to
quitting	stopped	park	barked	the	is
getting	hugged	yard	bark		
begged					

Dad made Arty a black cart.

"Can I drive at the park?" begged Arty.

"No. Drive in the yard," said Dad.

1

"I'm not quitting," Arty yelled to Dad.

"Marny is getting in the cart."

This time he had a happy bark!

4

Arty began humming.

He grabbed the wheel and
stepped on the gas.

The cart started!

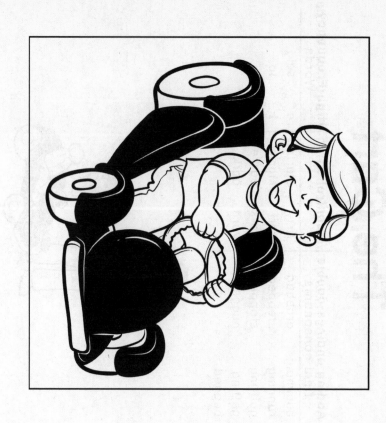

Marny the dog began running
beside Arty.

He barked a sad bark.

Arty stopped the cart and
hugged Marny.

© Pearson Education, Inc., 1

© Pearson Education, Inc., 1

Fern and Kurt grinned.

"We're glad to help.

Then you'll get to play a game with us!"

4

Name _____

Helping Mom

r-controlled *er, ir, ur*		Contractions	High-Frequency Words	
Fern	bird	I've	said	to
her	stir	I'll	the	play
shirts	fur	can't	I	
skirts	Kurt	we're	you	
dirty	burn	you'll	is	

"I've got sixteen jobs on my list," said Mom.

"I'll need all the help I can get."

1

"Fern, will you hang up these
shirts and skirts?" asked Mom.

"Will you brush the dog? Her fur
is dirty."

"Kurt, will you feed the bird?"
asked Mom.

"Will you stir the gumbo?
We can't let it burn."

© Pearson Education, Inc., 1

Name _____

The Contest

Comparative Endings -er and -est	Consonant Pattern -dge	High-Frequency Words	
bigger	hardest	judge	have	the
harder	darkest	edge	a	is
biggest	sharpest	fudge	said	

"Let's have a contest," said Bart.

"Jess will be the judge."

Sit on the edge, Jess."

© Pearson Education, Inc., 1

"My fudge is darkest," said Jess.

"My pencil is sharpest."

"You're not the judge anymore!" said Bart.

Decodable Story *The Contest*
Target Skill Comparative Endings *-er* and *-est*, Consonant Pattern *-dge*

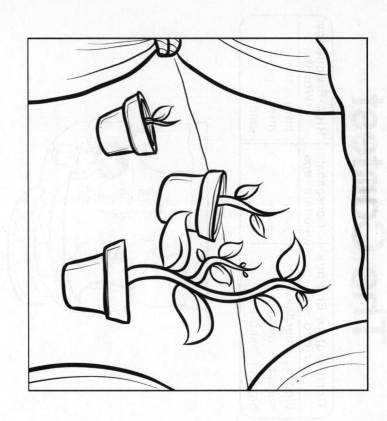

"My plant is big," said Bart.

"My plant is bigger than that plant," said Sandy.

"Mine is the biggest," said Jess.

"See this hard trick?" said Bart.

"My trick is harder," said Sandy.

"My trick is the hardest yet," said Jess.

© Pearson Education, Inc., 1

Name _____

Quails

Vowel Digraphs *ai, ay*		Singular and Plural Possessives	High-Frequency Words	
quails	stay	birds'	are	what
main	say	farmers'	their	do
trail	may	quail's	is	one
raid	someday		the	you
gray			many	a
			live	

Quails are small, plump birds.

Quails can fly, but their main home is on land.

© Pearson Education, Inc., 1

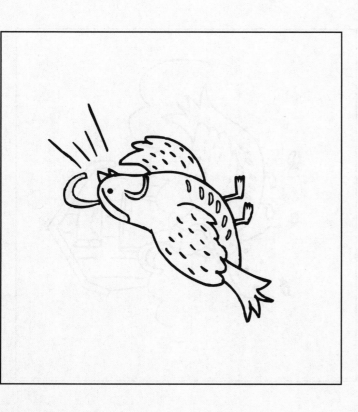

What do quails say?

One quail's call is *bob . . . WHITE!*

You may see a bobwhite someday!

Many quails are tan, gray, and white.

The birds' spots and stripes help them hide.

They run up the trail when foxes raid.

2

Quails can live on farmers' farms.

They like seeds and insects. Farmers hope the quails will stay!

© Pearson Education, Inc., 1

3

Name _____

Bread

Vowel Digraph *ea*		Adding Endings: Change *y* to *i*	High-Frequency Words	
bread	yeast	babies	a	I
eat	treat	ladies	your	the
feast	leave	dried	are	is
wheat	meal	fried	you	
read	clean	tried	about	
beat			said	

© Pearson Education, Inc., 1

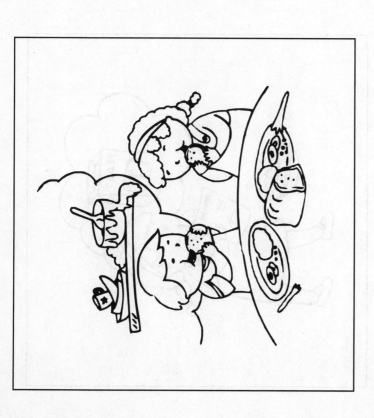

"This is a treat!" said Beth.

"But I must leave after the meal."

"No . . . after we clean up!" said Neal.

"Babies like it! Ladies like it!"

Eat it with jelly!

It's a feast in your belly!" sang Neal.

1

4

"Are you singing about bread?"
asked Beth.

"Yes!" said Neal. "I'm mixing the
wheat bread.

Will you help me?"

"I've never tried that before,"
said Beth.

"But I can read the card.

I'll beat in the yeast."

© Pearson Education, Inc., 1

Name _____

It's Spring!

Vowel Digraphs oa, ow			3-Letter Consonant Blends, Including thr, spl		High-Frequency Words	
toad	snow	show	spring	thrill	the	a
croaks	crow	throw	splash	street	what	your
boat	flowers	yellow	sprout		do	out
goat	row		stream		you	is
oats	grow		stretch		to	

The snow went away. It's spring!

The crow flies. The toad croaks.

The fish splash. The flowers sprout.

1

Spring is a thrill!

Spring is the best season on my street ... until summer, that is!

4

© Pearson Education, Inc., 1

Decodable Story *It's Spring!*
Target Skills Vowel Digraphs *oa, ow*; 3-Letter Consonant Blends, Including *thr, spl*

167

What do you like to do in spring?

You can row a boat up the stream.

You can grow a rose.

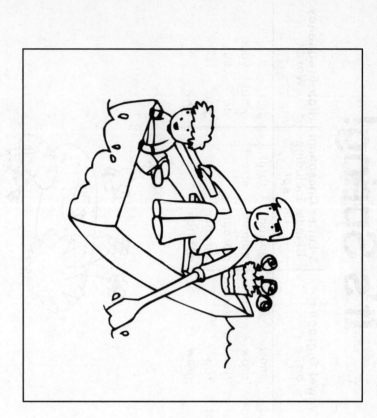

You can throw a ball to a pal.

You can feed oats to the goat.

You can stretch out on the grass.

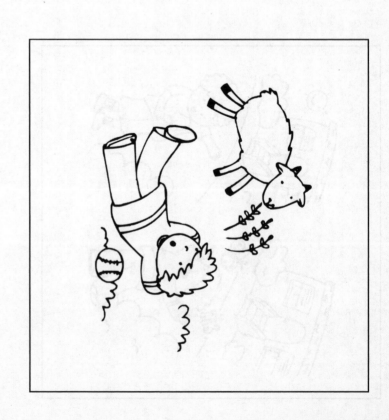

© Pearson Education, Inc., 1

Name _____

The Gift

Vowel Digraphs *ie, igh*		Consonant Patterns *kn, wr*		High-Frequency Words	
brief	might	knee	wrench	a	were
chief	right	kneeled	wrapped	the	is
necktie	bright	knot		was	what
ties	tight	know		to	do
tie	sighed	wrong		said	too
night					

Carl went on a brief shopping trip.

The chief reason was to get a gift.

His dad's birthday party was that night.

© Pearson Education, Inc., 1

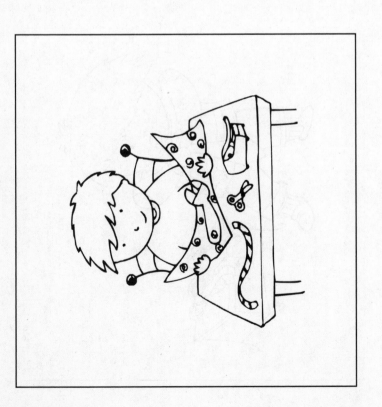

Carl didn't know what to do.

Then he got a wrench instead.

He wrapped it. Dad liked it!

4

"Dad might like a necktie," said
Carl.

The ties were right by his knee.

Carl kneeled to see.

2

© Pearson Education, Inc., 1

Carl tried on a bright red tie.

He made the knot too tight.

"This is all wrong!" he sighed.

3

© Pearson Education, Inc., 1

Name _____

Sue's Daydream

Compound Words		Vowel Digraphs ue, ew, ui		High-Frequency Words	
daydream	sunlight	Sue	crew	was	I
daydreaming	inside	true	Drew	a	to
onto	popcorn	blue	juice	the	
suitcase	everyone	new	cruise	they	
into	herself	flew		said	

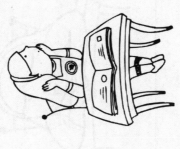

Sue was in reading class,

but she wasn't reading.

It's true—Sue was daydreaming!

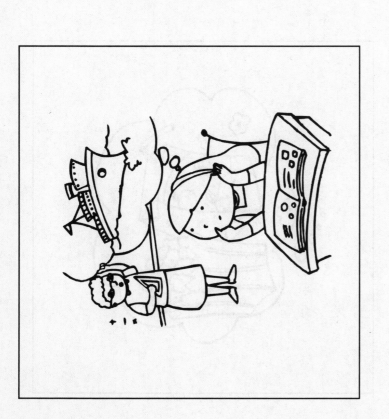

"Time for math!" said Miss Drew.

"I must quit daydreaming," Sue said to herself.

"But a cruise might be fun . . ."

4

Decodable Story *Sue's Daydream*
Target Skills Compound Words; Vowel Digraphs *ue, ew, ui*

She got onto a plane with her new suitcase.

The plane flew off into the blue sky.

Sunlight streamed in.

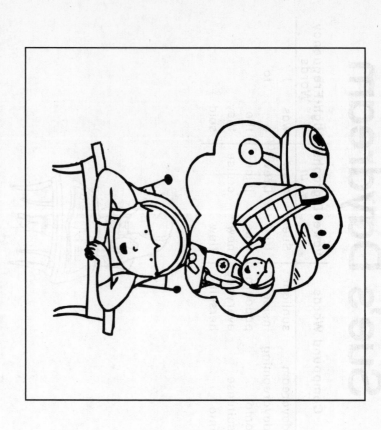

© Pearson Education, Inc., 1

The crew inside was nice.

"We've got juice and popcorn for everyone," they said.

© Pearson Education, Inc., 1

Name _____

Helping at a Zoo

Suffixes -ly, -ful	Vowel Sound in moon: oo	High-Frequency Words	
mainly	zoo	cool	a	some
quickly	bloom	soon	many	visit
likely	food	too	people	you
playful	broom	booth		
painful				

Many people help at a zoo.

Some mainly help flowers bloom.

Some get food for everyone.

You'll likely visit a zoo someday.

Will you go soon?

Will you help at a zoo too?

Decodable Story *Helping at a Zoo*
Target Skills Suffixes -ly, -ful; Vowel Sound in *moon: oo*

Some helpers use a broom all day.

Some helpers sell treats in a booth.

Some helpers keep playful hippos cool.

© Pearson Education, Inc., 1

A vet helps at a zoo.
A cub might get a painful cut.
A vet quickly helps its cut heal.

Name _____

Chow

Diphthongs ow and ou		Final Syllable -le	High-Frequency Words
Chow	ground	little	was
how	around	beagle	a
bow	grouch	tumble	said
now	sound	Mingle	I
howl	loud	puddle	the
scowled	found	nibble	to
growl		chuckle	is
stout			
hound			
proud			

Chow was a stout little beagle.

"See how my hound can tumble and bow?" said Miss Mingle. "I am proud!"

© Pearson Education, Inc., 1

Then Miss Mingle got Chow a treat.

"Nibble this," she said with a chuckle.

"Now we'll all feel better!"

4

Decodable Story Chow
Target Skills Diphthongs ow and ou, Final Syllable -le

Chow found a puddle on the ground.
He splashed mud all around.
"Now I am a grouch!" said Miss Mingle.

Chow started to howl.
"That sound is too loud," Miss Mingle scowled.
"Everyone in town will growl!" Mingle.

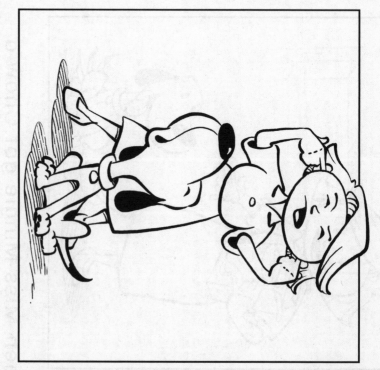

© Pearson Education, Inc., 1

3

176

A New Home

Vowel Patterns *ow* (how)(show), *ou*		Syllables V/CV and VC/V		High-Frequency Words	
brown	windows	found	Toby's	city	a	is
now	throw	house	tiny	models	I	of
down	yellow	out	begin	comics	the	to
town	pillow		baby	closet	said	their
			label			

Toby's dad got a new job.

"I found a brown house in the city," he said.

"It is tiny, but it has lots of windows."

1

© Pearson Education, Inc., 1

Dad and Toby missed their house in town.

But Dad liked his new job, and Toby liked his shiny new closet!

4

"I'll begin to pack right now,"
said Toby.

"I'll throw out my yellow baby
pillow,

but I'll pack my models and
comics!"

2

"I'll label the boxes," said Dad.

"We'll take them down to the
truck."

© Pearson Education, Inc., 1

3

Going for a Drive

Vowel Sound in *foot: oo*	Drop Final *e* to Add Endings		High-Frequency Words	
stood	smiling	saving	was	what
good	driving	piling	a	to
shook	taking	riding	said	I
cookies	baking	waving	their	go
cookbook	writing		the	
look				

Dad was smiling. He stood up.

"It's a good day for driving," he said.

"I'm taking everyone with me. Let's go!"

1

© Pearson Education, Inc., 1

"We're piling in the car and riding downtown," said Dad, waving at the kids.

"I know just the place to go!"

4

Lacy and Mike shook their heads.

"We're baking cookies, but we can't find the cookbook."

© Pearson Education, Inc., 1

Jon and Margo shook their heads.

"We're writing about saving the whales, but we don't know what to look up."

© Pearson Education, Inc., 1

Name _____

What Are You?

Diphthongs oi, oy	Suffixes -er, -or		High-Frequency Words
soil	reader	singer	a
coins	writer	actor	are
boy	talker	baker	you
toy	dreamer	maker	do
joy	runner	farmer	the
	skater	banker	many

You're a boy or girl.

You're a reader and writer.

You're a talker and dreamer.

4

You are good at many things.

Try new things.

Keep doing the things that bring you joy!

Are you a fast runner or skater?

Are you a good singer or actor?

Are you a baker or toy maker?

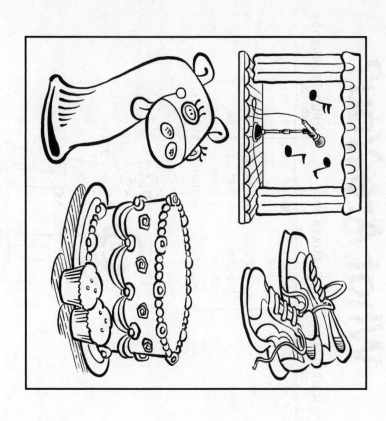

© Pearson Education, Inc., 1

Do you like the soil?

Do you collect coins?

Will you be a farmer or a banker?

Paul Bunyan

Vowel Sound *aw, au*		Syllable Patterns: Digraphs and Diphthongs		High Frequency Words	
Paul	sawed	boyhood	sailboats	a	of
yawned	Paul's	football	oatmeal	was	other
dawn	straw		seacoast	as	do
				the	

People tell tall tales about Paul Bunyan.

Paul had quite a boyhood.

His room was as big as ten football fields.

© Pearson Education, Inc., 1

Paul had a blue ox named Babe.

Babe ate thirty bales of straw for a snack.

What other tall tales do people tell?

4

Paul liked to look at the seacoast.

When Paul yawned, he slurped the sailboats right out of the sea.

Paul ate nine bathtubs of oatmeal each dawn.

Then Paul and his dad sawed wood.

Paul was a hard worker.

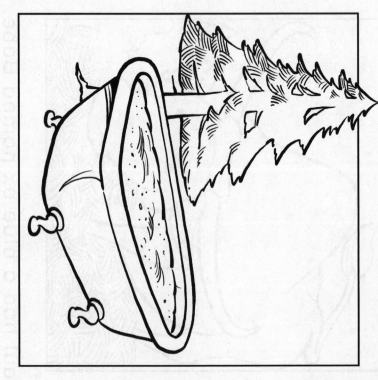

© Pearson Education, Inc., 1

Name _____

Quincy's Bad Day

Prefixes *un-* and *re-*	Long *o* and Long *i*		High-Frequency Words		
unhappy	told	wild	you	the	
unlocked	sold	kind	I	to	
unwise	old	find	said	your	
replace	folded		a	some	
restart	most				

"You look most unhappy," Jess told Quincy.

"I AM unhappy," Quincy said.

"Why?" asked Jess with a kind smile.

© Pearson Education, Inc., 1

Jess folded her arms.

"It's unwise to stay sad," she said. "Let's restart your day and have some fun!"

4

"First, Dad sold my old bike.
"I hope I can replace it."

© Pearson Education, Inc., 1

"Then, the dog went wild.
He ran out the unlocked gate.
I didn't find him until just now."